Also by Jan Henson Dow

Nonfiction
Writing the Award-Winning Play (with Shannon Michal Dow.)

Poetry
At the Han-ku Pass

Short Plays
Plays that Pop!: One-Act, Ten-Minute, and Monologues

Full-Length Plays
Dark Passages (with Shannon Michal Dow and Robert Schroeder, published by Popular Play Service.)
Dreamers, Shadows, Dreams (with Robert Schroeder, published by Phosphene Publishing Co.)
The Golden Dawn (with Robert Schroeder, published by Phosphene Publishing Co.)
Killing Dante (with Shannon Michal Dow, published by Samuel French, Inc.)
The Magistry (with Robert Schroeder, published by Popular Play Service.)
The Moorlark (with Shannon Michal Dow, published by Phosphene Publishing Co.)
Shaka (with Robert Schroeder, published by Phosphene Publishing Co.)
That Madcap Moon (with Robert Schroeder, published by Phosphene Publishing Co.)

Dreamers, Shadows, Dreams

Dreamers, Shadows, Dreams

A Play by

Jan Henson Dow
&
Robert Schroeder

Phosphene Publishing Company
Houston, Texas

Dreamers, Shadows, Dreams
© 2017 by Jan Henson Dow
ISBN 10: 0-9986316-2-0
ISBN 13: 978-0-9986316-2-2

This play is a work of fiction. Names, characters, places, and incidents either are products of the author's imagination or are used as fiction.

All rights reserved. No part of this work may be copied or otherwise produced or reproduced in any form—printed, electronic, live performance, videotaping, recording, or otherwise—without express permission of Phosphene Publishing Company, except for brief excerpts used in reviews, articles, and critical works.

Published by
Phosphene Publishing Company
Houston, Texas, USA
phosphenepublishing.com

To the memory of my dear friend

Mildred House Shrader

Production of Dreamers, Shadows, Dreams

This edition of *Dreamers, Shadows, Dreams* is dedicated to the reading public only. Professionals and amateurs are hereby warned that the play is subject to production fees. All rights, including professional, amateur, motion pictures, recitation, lecturing, public reading, radio broadcasting, television, and the rights of translation into foreign languages, are strictly reserved.

The amateur live stage performance rights to *Dreamers, Shadows, Dreams* are controlled exclusively by Phosphene Publishing Company. There is a fee of $35 to produce this play, and the fee must be paid and rights secured in writing from Phosphene Publishing Company at least two weeks prior to the opening performance of the play. The fee must be paid whether the play is presented for charity or by a nonprofit or profit-seeking organization and whether or not admission is charged.

Professional and stock royalty will be quoted on application to Phosphene Publishing Company.

Copying from this book without express permission of the publisher is strictly forbidden by law, and the right of performance is not transferable.

Whenever the play is produced, the following notice must appear on all programs, printing, and advertising for the play: "Produced by special arrangement with Phosphene Publishing Company."

Due authorship credit must be given on all programs, printing, and advertising for the play.

No one shall commit or authorize any act or omission by which the copyright, or the right to copyright, of this play may be impaired.

No one may make any changes to this play in the process of production, or otherwise.

Correspondence and inquiries may be made through the Phosphene Publishing Company website at phosphenepublishing.com.

Dreamers, Shadows, Dreams

Cast of Characters

JENNIFER is an attractive woman in her forties. Her dark hair has no touch of gray, and her figure is slim and youthful. Her dress is simple, becoming, and understated.

JENNY (Jennifer as a girl) is 15, slim and pretty, with long, dark hair. SHE is wearing a skirt, sweater, saddle shoes, and white bobby socks.

CHRISTINE appears to be about 17 years old and dressed as she appears in the past. Her face is thoughtful and solemn in repose.

CHRIS (Christine as a girl) is about 17 She is a pretty girl with light brown hair worn pulled up and soft about her face. Although Chris and Christine are played by two actresses, both should be similar in appearance due to their similar ages.

LENA KRAUS is a woman in her 40s. Her complexion has an unhealthy pallor. Her hair is in an untidy bun. She wears an old house dress, loose, unbecoming, and shapeless, and old house slippers. Her movements Are slow and somnambulistic, her eyes staring straight ahead, as if fixed. She shifts their focus by slowly moving her whole body.

WALTER KRAUS is in his middle 40s, but looks older. He is ungainly and clumsy, and his coarse face is the result of many years of heavy drinking. He wears dark, baggy trousers with suspenders and a wrinkled white shirt without a tie.

JORDAN is about 40, tall and distinguished looking.

FRANK is played by same actor who plays Jordan. As Frank, he stands in a spotlight with his back to the audience.

DORINE, in her late 30s to mid 40s, is African American. She is sweet faced and plump with a warm, motherly manner. She is dressed in a blue uniform and low, white, comfortable shoes.

Set

The main set is the interior of the Kraus home in a small town in Kentucky in 1947. It is not a realistic set, but as if composed of memory and dream. The set has three main areas:

- UR is the suggestion of a living room containing a sofa, a coffee table, a rocking chair, and a lamp. A window is indicated at the upstage wall. There is a door to an unseen shop at R.
- UC is the suggestion of the parents' bedroom with a bed and dresser, its floor higher than the main stage floor. A door at center stage L opens from the kitchen into an unseen hall.
- UL is the suggestion of a kitchen, containing an ice box, a sink, a period gas stove, and a cupboard. A table and three chairs are DL of center, in the kitchen area, and there is a phone on the wall. An "outside" door leading to a porch is DL. Chris' books are on the table.

Dreamers, Shadows, Dreams

ACT I: SCENE ONE

(LIGHTS RISE on Jennifer's bedroom in Connecticut DL and also DC. The time is the 1980's. JENNIFER is standing DR. The telephone on a table DL starts to RING. JENNIFER crosses to answer it, hesitates, and stops without answering the phone.)

JENNIFER

No! No! Don't be a fool!
    (The telephone RINGS five times.)
It's too late. Oh, Jordan, don't call me anymore!
    (The telephone STOPS ringing. SHE paces, as if in a panic, trying to escape.)
Is anyone there? Anyone there? They are all gone: my mother, my father, my lover, my child.
    (Pause.)
Christine! I could always talk to Christine! It's been a long time, but she would understand. Christine will understand.

(As if picking up the phone and calling. DIM SPOT, UR. FRANK stands in SPOT with his back to the audience.)

FRANK

Hello.

JENNIFER

Hello—Frank? It's Jenny.

FRANK

Jenny? It's been a long time.

JENNIFER

Yes, I've meant to call, but so much has happened. Time goes by so quickly. May I speak to Christine?

FRANK

I'm sorry. Christine is—too ill to come to the phone.

JENNIFER

Frank, what is it? What's happened?

FRANK

Christine is—dying.

JENNIFER

Oh, my God! Oh, no! What...dying?

FRANK

She doesn't have much longer. They diagnosed a brain tumor—a month ago.

JENNIFER

A month ago? Oh, no!

FRANK

She's so weak now—too weak to lift a glass of water. She's prayed for death.

JENNIFER

Oh, Frank—if there's anything I can do....

FRANK

Earlier she asked for you, but she wouldn't know you now.

JENNIFER

Wouldn't know me? Oh, Frank, if there's any change—if you want me to come....

FRANK

I'll let you know. I'll call you.

(SPOT, UR, goes DARK.)

JENNIFER

She wouldn't know me now.... Oh, Christine!—Christine!

(SHE hangs up the phone and sits in an attitude of despair, her hands covering her eyes. The light FADES, indicating the real world is giving way to a dream world. A SPOT slowly RISES, DR. CHRISTINE appears in the SPOT. She is looking across the stage at JENNIFER. Her face is thoughtful and solemn in repose. JENNIFER looks across the stage at CHRISTINE. JENNIFER slowly stands and looks at CHRISTINE more intently as if trying to discover who the figure is. Throughout this sequence, JENNIFER and CHRISTINE maintain their positions on opposite sides of the stage.)

CHRISTINE

Jenny.

JENNIFER

Who is it? Chris—is it you? Is it really you?

CHRISTINE

Yes.

JENNIFER

Then—you didn't die!

CHRISTINE

I died—and I am here.

JENNIFER

Here?

CHRISTINE

You are asleep and dreaming.

JENNIFER

Asleep? Dreaming?

CHRISTINE

I am sharing your dream

JENNIFER

But you died of cancer. You died a painful and horrible death. At the end, you prayed for death.
   (Pause.)
Don't you remember your death? Don't you remember the pain?

CHRISTINE

I have forgotten.

JENNIFER

I haven't forgotten you, Christine. You were the best friend I ever had! We were like—sisters.

CHRISTINE

Yes—we were like sisters.

JENNIFER

We shared everything.

CHRISTINE

Yes—we shared everything.

JENNIFER

(Reaching toward CHRISTINE as if wanting to move but unable to do so.)

Oh, Christine, I didn't come to you when you were dying. I didn't come to your funeral! I couldn't face your death.

CHRISTINE

You are here now.

(SPOT FADES on CHRISTINE. The SPOT on JENNIFER slowly FADES to BLACKOUT. LIGHTING COMES UP on the interior of the main set: the Kraus home in a small town in Kentucky. It is not a realistic set but as if composed of memory and dream. The year is 1947. The set has three main areas: living room UR, parents' bedroom UC, and kitchen UL. A door to an unseen shop is at R. An "outside" door leading to a porch is DL. Chris' books are on the table. CHRIS crosses to the sink and begins to dry the dishes. LENA is standing in the kitchen, looking out over the audience as if looking out a window. SHE stands with her hands at her sides, her movements slow and somnambulistic, her eyes staring straight ahead, as if fixed. She shifts their focus by slowly moving her whole body.)

CHRIS

There, that's done. Mother, go on in and listen to the radio. Jenny is coming over, and we're going to make some fudge and do our homework.

(LENA does not seem to hear or move)

LENA

It's going to rain. We are all going to die.

CHRIS

For God's sake, Mother! Isn't there any privacy in this house? Go on into the living room!
   (CHRIS pushes LENA toward the living room.)
Go on and listen to the radio.

LENA

Can I have some fudge?

CHRIS

Yes, of course. I'll bring you a plate when it's done.

   (LENA slowly crosses to a position upstage in the living room, where she stands, her back to the audience, looking out the window. CHRIS crosses to the kitchen and begins to mix the fudge in a pan on the stove. JENNY (Jennifer at age 15), carrying her books, enters the living room from the unseen shop R. SHE wears a skirt, sweater, saddle shoes, and white bobby socks.)

WALTER (VOICE OFF)

(In a tipsy voice.)
Tell Christine to get on out here. I need her to help. Tell her to get on out here.

JENNY

I'll tell her, Mr. Kraus.
  (Seeing LENA.)
Hello, Miz Kraus. How're you feeling?

   (LENA turns slowly in JENNY'S direction but does not immediately recognize her.)

LENA

Is it—Jenny?

JENNY

Yes, ma'am.
>(Pause.)
Mother said to tell you she hopes you're feeling better.

LENA

Your mother is kind. She is a kind woman.

JENNY

Yes, ma'am. Is Chris home?
>(LENA does not answer but stiffly turns back to the window.)

Well, I'll just go on back.
>(JENNY crosses to the kitchen.)

Hi, Chris, I'm here.

CHRIS

I've started the fudge.

JENNY

>(Putting her books on the table.)

Your father said to tell you to get on out there.

CHRIS

>(Calmly continuing to stir the fudge.)

Don't listen to him. You know how he is when he gets like that. Dorine will close up the shop.

JENNY

Is your mother going into one of her spells again? She seems sort of far away.

CHRIS
My God! One of these days she's going to drive me as crazy as she is!

JENNY
You'll never be crazy. You're the sanest person I know. You can do anything! Cook, sew, clean—there isn't anything you can't do! I don't know how to do anything practical at all.

CHRIS
That's because you don't have to know how to do anything. You have Lafronia and Jeff to do the chores. And anything they don't do for you, your mother does. She never makes you do anything.

JENNY
I hate to be made to do things. I don't want to ever have to do anything.

CHRIS
Well, your mother has never made you do anything that I know of.

JENNY
I know, and I would hate it if she did.

CHRIS
I wouldn't worry if I were you.

JENNY
I love my mother more than anybody. It's just that I can't talk to her at all. She isn't a bit smart. My father's smart, but I can't talk to him either. I always come to you when I need someone to talk to. Is the fudge ready yet?

CHRIS
In a minute. We'll let it set while we do our homework.

JENNY
(Sitting at the table.)
Okay.

WALTER
(Leaning into the living room from the shop door R and shouting in an alcoholic voice.)
Christine! Christine! Get on out here and close up the shop!

CHRIS
Just ignore him. Maybe he'll shut up and go back into the shop.

WALTER
(Entering the living room.)
Christine! Come on out here!

CHRIS
Sh-h-h. Don't say anything.

WALTER
(Crossing to the kitchen.)
Didn't you hear me calling?

CHRIS
I heard you. The whole neighborhood heard you. I'm making fudge, and then we're going to do our homework.

WALTER
I'm not feeling well. I want you to come on out and close up the shop.

CHRIS
Well, who would feel well after drinking as much as you do? You know Dorine will close up. She always does.

WALTER
You don't care a thing about me. Nobody cares. I could live or die. Nobody cares.

CHRIS
Jenny, stir this so it won't burn.

(As JENNY stirs the fudge, CHRIS crosses to WALTER and gives him a hug.)

I do care about you, Daddy. I love you. You know that. But I'm not going to come running every time you call. I'd never get anything else done. Now go on and lie down on the sofa and rest. Dorine will close up. She always does.

(CHRIS helps WALTER cross into the living room to the sofa.)

WALTER
(To LENA.)
Why are you always standing around, you ugly, old bitch?

CHRIS

Hush, for God's sake!

(WALTER reaches for a the butt of a cigar in an ashtray on the coffee table and makes a fumbling attempt to light it. CHRIS takes the cigar away from HIM and returns it to the ashtray)

And don't light that cigar! You'll fall asleep and set the whole house on fire!

WALTER
(Lying on the sofa.)
I guess I don't need you telling me what to do in my own house.

CHRIS

Mother, go on into the bedroom. Go on now. You'll only get him upset if you stay here. Go on and lie down.

LENA

Is Jenny here?

CHRIS

Yes, now go on.

>   (CHRIS begins to shove LENA gently. They cross
>   to the UC bedroom where LENA sits on the bed.)

LENA

Can I have some fudge?

CHRIS

I told you I'd bring you some when it's ready. Now lie down and rest.
>   (As CHRIS crosses into the kitchen, WALTER
>   lights the cigar and lies down on the sofa, blowing
>   smoke rings.)

I guess we can have some peace and quiet now.

JENNY

>   (Still stirring the fudge.)

You have to do everything around here. How can you stand it? Is this done?

CHRIS

Yes, it's ready. We'll pour it in this pan and let it set. Here. You can lick the spoon.

>   (CHRIS gives JENNY the spoon and then with a
>   second spoon scrapes the fudge into a flat, square
>   pan then puts the pan into the ice box.)

JENNY

>   (Licking the spoon.)

I love chocolate fudge even if it does make me break out.

CHRIS and JENNY

>   (BOTH licking their spoons.)

M–m–m–m–m!

CHRIS

I have to study my French. I have a test tomorrow.

JENNY
Let's not study. I don't want to study. I don't like to study.

CHRIS
How would you know whether you like it or not? I've never seen you study anything.

JENNY
I don't need to study. I'm just naturally smart.

CHRIS
Well, Miss Smarty Pants, I guess I'm not as smart as you are.

JENNY
Let's talk or read poetry.

CHRIS
When I've finished studying, we'll read something together.

JENNY
(Sitting at the table, disinterestedly turns the pages of a book.)
Okay.

(CHRIS sits at the table and begins to study. SPOT COMES UP on JENNIFER, DL, and on CHRISTINE who remains seated. JENNIFER is looking at CHRISTINE as if from afar. CHRISTINE raises her head but does not turn to look at JENNIFER.)

JENNIFER
Oh, Christine, how young we were then.

CHRISTINE
Yes, Jenny, we were young then.

JENNIFER

What dreams we had. You were going to be a great artist and I was going to be a great poet.
        (Pause.)
But you married and had children, and you died young.

CHRISTINE

Yes.

JENNIFER

Oh, Christine, what happened to our dreams?

CHRISTINE

They are here with us now.

        (LIGHTS FADE on the Kraus household. A SPOT RISES, DL. SOUND of the rain falling.)

JENNIFER

        (Raises an umbrella and stands, as if in the rain.)
The night that I went to the reception at The Players Club, it was raining. I almost decided not to go. It seemed so strange to go without Paul, without a husband. Strange after all these years together. Don't be a fool, I thought. You've got to start going out sometime. No one will lead you by the hand.
        (SHE closes the umbrella and puts it down. SHE turns toward DL where JORDAN is standing, with a drink in HIS hand.)
The room was crowded with people. Strange faces in a crowded room, but it was as if I was looking for someone. "I don't really know anyone." I thought. "But why do I feel I'm looking for someone?" I turned and looked across the room, and he was standing there, against the wall, a drink in his hand— a little space all around him. I knew I had to go and meet him. "He's probably married and has six children," I thought. "But I've got to go and meet him." I walked across the room.

(SHE crosses as few steps DL to where JORDAN is standing.)

"Hello," I said.

JORDAN

Hello.

JENNIFER

He looked at me—no—that's not the right word. He—knew me. Oh, I don't mean that we had met before. I mean that he knew me and I knew him. As if we had always known each other.
(To JORDAN.)
Forgive me, I know we haven't met....

JORDAN

No, you're wrong. We have met.

JENNIFER

But we don't know each other.

JORDAN

Yes—we do know each other. I just don't know your name.

JENNIFER

Jennifer.

JORDAN

Jennifer—yes—Jordan. Let me get you a drink. What would you like?

JENNIFER

"I don't know," I said. I felt confused—not thinking clearly.

JORDAN

A dry vermouth on the rocks.

JENNIFER

Yes, I'd like that.

JORDAN

Stay right there. Don't move. Promise.

JENNIFER

I promise.

JORDAN

I don't want to lose you.

(HE turns and crosses L. DL SPOT begins to FADE.)

JENNIFER

I watched him make his way through the crowd. He stood at the bar, taller than anyone else—and even in that crowd, keeping a little space around him. I waited for him as if I had always been waiting for him to come back. As if I would always wait for him to come back, whatever happened.

(SPOT FADES on JENNIFER as she exits. DORINE enters the living room from the shop door at R and crosses to the sofa, where WALTER is dozing. She takes his cigar out of his hand and puts it in the ash tray. She shakes him gently.)

DORINE

Walter...! Walter! I'm almost ready to go on home. Anything else you want 'fore I close up the shop?

WALTER

Count the money in the register.

DORINE

Don't I always?
>(To CHRIS.)
Honey, I'm 'bout ready to go.

>(SHE crosses to CHRIS and looks over CHRIS' shoulder.)

CHRIS

If you stay a while, you can have some fudge.

DORINE

I cain't. I got to go fix Clarence's supper. He gets mighty peeved if he don't get his supper on time. You save me some of that fudge for tomorrow, you hear?

>(DORINE stands beside CHRIS with her hand on CHRIS' shoulder. CHRIS puts her hand over DORINE'S.)

CHRIS

I will—if Jenny doesn't eat it all.

JENNY

I love fudge.

DORINE

What you all doin'?

CHRIS

Studying French.

DORINE

You all are mighty smart. Is that somethin' like English?

CHRIS
Something like.

DORINE
Hm–m–m–m, French do look hard. How's your mother, Jenny?

JENNY
She's fine.

DORINE
She's a sweet woman, you mother. She got a good heart. Even if she do spoil you rotten.

JENNY
I'm not spoiled, Dorine.

DORINE
Yes, you is, honey. You's the spoilest child I know. But you got her same sweet smile.

JENNY
I don't look a thing like my momma.

DORINE
Yes, you do. But you proud like you daddy. How's Jeff and Lafronia?

JENNY
Lafronia says she's got the rheumatism.

DORINE
She got the old age creepin' up, that's what she got. Lord, don't we all. I better go on and close up the shop. I got to get on down the road. Clarence'll have a fit.

(DORINE crosses to LENA, preparing LENA for the night.)

JENNY

Is Dorine married to Clarence?

CHRIS

I think they just live together. Sometimes he beats her.

JENNY

That's terrible! I couldn't stand for anyone to beat me. I think I'd kill them before I'd let them beat me!

CHRIS

Sometimes she comes in with her eye all black and blue or a bruise on her face.

JENNY

What does she say?

CHRIS

All she says is, "That Clarence, he's a mean man when he's been drinkin'."

DORINE

(Reentering the kitchen area.)

I hear that! Don't you think I got ears? I makes do with what I got! And Clarence is what I got. Yes, Lord, Clarence is all I got! He's a lovin' man—when he's sober. I got to get on down the road, or Clarence'll have a fit.

(DORINE crosses and exits through the shop door R.)

CHRIS

I used to think the safest place in the world was in Dorine's lap and nothing could harm me there. She nursed me when I was little and my mother first got sick. Dorine was my real mother. I've always loved her more than that mother.

(LENA is clearly within hearing range and seems to be listening but shows no reaction.)

JENNY

I couldn't love anyone more than my mother! Don't you love your mother, Chris?

CHRIS

No. I think I hate her.

JENNY

Oh, Chris, don't say that! She might hear you. Does she know that you don't love her?

CHRIS

She doesn't know anything. She's too dumb.
        (LENA slowly, stiffly, puts her hand to her mouth in a gesture of silent anguish.)
Let's be quiet now so I can study. I have a test tomorrow, remember?

JENNY

Okay.

(THEY concentrate on their books. LIGHTS FADE on main set. SPOTS RISE DL and on CHRISTINE. JENNIFER at L is looking at CHRIS and JENNY. CHRISTINE raises her head but does not turn to look at JENNIFER.)

JENNIFER

Oh, Christine, it's you and I when we were young. But they don't know that we are here.

CHRISTINE

No, they can't see us.

JENNIFER
(Looking at LENA.)
Can your mother see us?

CHRISTINE
Yes, she can see us.

JENNIFER
She was standing by the door, listening. She must have heard everything. You said you didn't love her.

CHRISTINE
Yes, she always heard everything and endured it in silence.

JENNIFER
Did you know that she heard? Did you know?

CHRISTINE
Yes, I knew, but always pretended that I didn't know, until even I believed that she did not hear or feel anything.

JENNIFER
Oh, no. How could she bear it?

CHRISTINE
There is nothing given to you that you cannot bear.

JENNIFER
Miz Kraus. Miz Kraus. It's me—Jenny.

LENA
Jenny?

JENNIFER
Christine is here.

LENA

Christine is dead.

JENNIFER

No! She is here with me now! Speak to her!

(LENA turns away and lies down on the bed.)

CHRISTINE

We never knew each other.

JENNIFER

Mr. Kraus! Mr. Kraus—Christine is here with me.

(WALTER stirs restlessly but does not speak.)

CHRISTINE

They are all sleeping.

JENNIFER

I don't understand.
(SHE begins to shiver.)
I'm cold. It must be going to rain.

(LIGHTS FADE on the Kraus household and a SPOT RISES DL on a table and two chairs. SOUND of the rain falling. JENNIFER opens the umbrella)

JENNIFER

The night I went to the reception, the night I met Jordan, it was raining.
(SHE crosses L and she and JORDAN stand under the umbrella together.)
We went to a restaurant in the Village with a tiny garden just outside the window and a fountain playing.

(THEY sit at a small table.)

There was music and candlelight and wine. We listened to the music, just looking into each other's eyes.

JORDAN

You have raindrops in your hair.

JENNIFER

Do I?

JORDAN

Yes, sparkling, like your eyes. You're beautiful in candlelight. Your eyes are glowing.

JENNIFER

I remember the touch of his hand on mine—warm and gentle. Always I remember the touch of his hand. Later, we went to a tiny theater—I can't remember the play—only the warmth of his hand and the look in his eyes. When the play was over, there was no thought that the evening would end—no thought that we would have to part. We walked out together into the rain.

> (JORDAN stands behind JENNIFER as if they are looking over the lights of the city)

His apartment was on the tenth floor. We stood at the window, looking out over the lights of the city. The rain had stopped. There was a touch of mist in the air and all the lights were glowing.

(To JORDAN.)

The city is beautiful at night. All the lights are glowing.

JORDAN

Yes. The rain has stopped. It's beautiful, here with you. I want you—now.

JENNIFER

"I'm not sure," I said. "I don't know."

JORDAN
Yes, you are sure. You do know.

JENNIFER
And I said, "Yes."

(HE turns HER to face him. They slowly kiss. LIGHTS FADE as THEY exit. DL SPOT FADES. LIGHTS RISE on the kitchen area.)

JENNY
(Looking up, restlessly, then shivering.)
Haven't you studied enough, Chris?

CHRIS
(Looking up from her books.)
You're shivering.

JENNY
I'm cold. It must be going to rain. Do you think the fudge is ready yet?

CHRIS
(SHE goes to the icebox and takes out the pan of fudge.)
Yes, it looks ready.

(SHE puts the pan on the table and cuts and serves the fudge.)

JENNY
M–m–m–m! It's delicious!

CHRIS
What do you want to read?

JENNY

Cyrano de Bergerac!

CHRIS

You always want to read Cyrano.

JENNY

I love Cyrano. He's my dream lover.

CHRIS

Well, okay then, we'll read Cyrano. Wait a minute. I'll just take this fudge to my mother.
   (SHE crosses to the upstage bedroom and leans over
   LENA who appears to be asleep. CHRIS crosses to
   the kitchen.)
I think she's asleep. I better not wake her.

JENNY

M–m–m–m! Do you think making love is as good as fudge?

CHRIS

   (Eating a piece of fudge.)
Nothing is as good as fudge!

JENNY

I love Cyrano! He's better than fudge! He always makes me laugh and then cry. I wonder—do real lovers make you laugh and cry like Cyrano? Does Frank make you laugh and cry?

CHRIS

Sometimes we laugh, but he never makes me cry.

JENNY

Mrs. Frank Owens. Mrs. Franklin Russell Owens.
   (After a pause, with a grand gesture.)
Mrs. Cyrano de Bergerac!

CHRIS

Madame de Bergerac.

JENNY

Madame de Bergerac! Oh, I like that. It sounds so—sophisticated! Madame de Bergerac! Do you love Frank as much as I love Cyrano?

CHRIS

Cyrano isn't a real person, so you can't compare the two. Cyrano is just a character in a play.

JENNY

No, he's more than that! I can't explain it. Some characters in a play seem more real than real life. Maybe—you and I are just characters in a play. Have you ever thought of that?

CHRIS

No, and I'm not going to think of that now. Sometimes your ideas make my head ache.

    (The phone RINGS. CHRIS answers the phone.)
Hello.... Yes, she's here. I'll call her.
    (Putting her hand over the mouth piece.)
It's for you. It's that Norman Holtzer.

JENNY

Norman Holtzer! Ugh! Tell him I'm not here.

CHRIS

But I just told him you were here.

JENNY

Well, tell him—I'm not here now! Tell him I've gone.

CHRIS

Jenny!

JENNY

Tell him I was slain in a sword fight, Cyrano at my side! Tell him anything.

CHRIS

Jenny! You tell him!

JENNY

No.

CHRIS
(Speaking into the phone in a very sweet voice.)
Norman, I'm sorry. I thought Jenny was still here, but she just left.... I don't know where she went, Norman.... What? The Navy? I—I'll tell her when I see her. Good luck!
(CHRIS hangs up the phone, then turns to JENNY.)
Jenny, he said he's going to join the Navy when he graduates!

JENNY

I know.

CHRIS

What do you mean, you know?

JENNY

He keeps calling me. He calls me every night. When he told me he was going to join the Navy, he asked would I wait for him. Wait for him? How can I wait for him? I've never even gone out with him.

CHRIS

What if he's in love with you? Think how he must feel.

JENNY
Well, I'm not in love with him. I don't even know him.

CHRIS
Then why didn't you just tell him to stop calling you?

JENNY
I like it when boys call me. I can't help it that they're always falling in love with me when I'm not in love with them.

CHRIS
You'll never fall in love that way.

JENNY
I don't know anything about falling in love, do you? Are you in love with Frank?

CHRIS
I don't know. I've never been in love before.

JENNY
Then how do you know when you're in love? I don't think I would know and wouldn't that be awful?

CHRIS
I guess it's just a feeling that you get that you can't describe.

JENNY
Do you think you'll marry Frank? Even if you don't know hardly anything about falling in love?

CHRIS
Maybe I know more about it than you think. I have a date with Frank on Saturday night. He thought you might like to go out with his friend Paul. He told Paul about you, and he wants to meet you.

JENNY
I know my father wouldn't let me go. He never lets me do anything!

CHRIS
You could tell your father it's a double date and you wouldn't be by yourself.

JENNY
That wouldn't make any difference. He thinks you're too old to be my friend—"too mature."

CHRIS
Your father doesn't like me or my family. He doesn't want us to be friends.

JENNY
He doesn't know you like I do, that's why. Anyhow, I don't care what he likes. He always tries to control me. I hate it! What does Paul look like?

CHRIS
He's not as tall as Frank, and he has blond hair and blue eyes.

JENNY
He doesn't sound anything like Cyrano.

CHRIS
Silly! You're not going to marry him. You're just going out with him. You can still be true to Cyrano.

JENNY
I don't want to marry just anyone. I want to fall madly in love and be a great poet like Cyrano and die tragically, but I don't want to marry just anyone. It seems too—mundane.

CHRIS
I wouldn't want you to do anything "mundane," Your Highness. But would you just consent to date a commoner as a gracious gesture? We'll have supper out at the lake and go dancing.

JENNY
Dancing! Oh, I love to dance! That sounds like fun! I'll go. I could hide on the floor in the back seat of the car as we make our getaway.

CHRIS
It's settled then. Go on and get Cyrano. He's sitting on the shelf, waiting for you.

> (JENNY exits as CHRIS gathers her books. DORINE enters from shop R. She is very upset.)

DORINE
Walter! Walter!

WALTER
I told you to go on.

DORINE
I know you told me. And now I'm tellin' you! You done took some money outta that register again when I told you and told you...!

WALTER
Now, Dorine....

DORINE
Don't you "Now, Dorine" me! I know what you done with that money—sent Lucas on over to Second Street for a bottle of that whiskey! It ain't right! It ain't right!

WALTER
Well, it's my money. Guess I can do what I want to with my own money.

DORINE
It's you money all right, but I got to make it add up! If you want to steal from you self, go on, but wait 'til I done addin' it up. That there register is short ten dollars!

WALTER
All right! All right! I took ten dollars. I won't do it again. Does that satisfy you?

DORINE
I'll believe that when I see it! Well, I got to go on. Here's the money, minus ten dollars!

WALTER
Just give it to Christine. And lock up as you go out.

DORINE
Don't I always?
> (JENNY enters from the hall carrying a copy of *Cyrano de Bergerac* as DORINE crosses to the kitchen and puts the money bag on the table.)

Good night, honey. See you all in the mornin'.

CHRIS
Good night, Dorine.

DORINE
Good night, Jenny.

JENNY
Good night, Dorine.

DORINE
(Crossing to LENA.)
Good night, Lena. See you all in the mornin'.

LENA
Dorine, they took all my pictures and tore them up.

DORINE
No, they didn't do no such thing. You pictures is right where they supposed to be, in this here drawer. Now, don't you worry 'bout them pictures none, you hear? Good night, honey.

>(SHE gives LENA a comforting pat on the shoulder and then exits.)

LENA
>(Speaking to no one.)

They took all my memories and tore them up, and all the pieces blew away in the wind.

CHRIS
>(To JENNY.)

What scene do you want to read?

JENNY
The last one, where Roxane discovers Cyrano has loved her all along, and then he dies. I'll be Cyrano.

CHRIS
That's the best part.

JENNY
I know. That's why I chose it. I don't like to play Roxane. She never gets to do anything exciting—like a sword fight. En garde!

>(JENNY thrusts with an imaginary sword, proclaiming in an exaggerated accent.)

Let me play zee part of Cyrano, or I run you through!

CHRIS
Help! I surrender! You can be Cyrano and I'll be Roxane.

JENNY
You take the book. I know the scene by heart.

(CHRIS, as Roxane, sits on a chair and JENNY, as Cyrano, enters. THEY are serious as they read the scene.)

CHRIS as Roxane
Ah, Cyrano, my old friend, you are late.

JENNY as Cyrano
(SHE kneels and kisses CHRIS'S hand.)
Forgive me, my dear Roxane, my dear friend. I was—detained.

(As if suddenly faint, JENNY as Cyrano falters and almost falls.)

CHRIS as Roxane
(Rising, frightened.)
My dear friend! You are so pale! Are you ill?

JENNY as Cyrano
(Sitting.)
Just—tired. My old wound. It's nothing. I'm all right.
(LIGHT begins to fade.)
Why is it growing so very dark?

(As if faint, SHE bows her head)

CHRIS as Roxane
(Going to HIS side.)
Oh, my dear, what is it? What is wrong?

JENNY as Cyrano
Farewell, my dear, dear friend.
No more shall I look upon your face
Or tell you of the love that we have shared.

CHRIS as Roxane

You speak in a voice that I have heard somewhere before. Yes, everything is clear. That night beneath my window—it was your voice speaking when I believed it was Christian's voice!

JENNY as Cyrano

No!

CHRIS as Roxane

And the words in Christian's letters were your words. Those words of love, all were yours!

JENNY as Cyrano

No!

CHRIS as Roxane

The words of love and loss were yours!

JENNY as Cyrano

My dear, my best beloved friend.

CHRIS as Roxane

Why has it taken all these years for you to speak? Why do you break your silence now, today?
(JENNY seems faint.)
Oh, no! You are wounded! What have they done to you?

JENNY as Cyrano

I thought to die a hero's death, with a jest on my lips and facing a noble foe. But look how I must die, my enemy unseen. What irony! To die and not know how or why. Farewell, my dear Roxane. The death bell tolls today must call me home.

CHRIS as Roxane

Oh, no!
(Calling offstage.)
Sister...! Sister...! I need your help!

JENNIFER

Sister...! Sister! I need your help!

CHRISTINE

Remember that we lived and loved each other, and love endures even beyond the grave.

(The faint sound of phone RINGING as if it is far away.)

CHRIS

(Crossing to the phone as if sleepwalking.)
Hello.... Yes, ma'am. She's here.
(Calling to JENNY.)
Jenny—Jenny.

(JENNY and JENNIFER'S body positions are identical, a stance of expectancy and yearning.)

JENNY and JENNIFER

Yes.

CHRIS

It's your mother calling.

JENNY and JENNIFER

Mother?

JENNY

Tell her I'm on my way home.

JENNIFER
Tell her I'm on my way home.

BLACKOUT

END OF SCENE ONE

ACT I: SCENE TWO

(SPOT RISES DL. JENNIFER is standing in the SPOT at DL.)

JENNIFER

The house silent and lonely when the echoes die away.
 (Pause.)
Is anyone there? Anyone there?
 (Pause.)
Oh, Jordan, I was afraid of loving and being loved. I never loved anyone before you. Not my husband, Paul, not anyone. They always loved me, but I never loved anyone before you. I've looked into the mirror of their eyes searching for that feeling I never had. They never knew me.
 (Pause.)
But when I looked into your eyes, there was no space between us anymore. Oh, Jordan, where are you? Where are you? Everything seems to be breaking up into pieces—like some crazy jigsaw puzzle I can't put back together. Where do I begin to fit the pieces together again? Christine? Are you there?

(SPOT UP on CHRISTINE DR.)

CHRISTINE

Yes, I am here.

JENNIFER

Is it still night?

CHRISTINE

Yes, it is still night.

JENNIFER

The house is so quiet. I feel so alone in the night.

CHRISTINE
I am here.

(SPOTS on CHRISTINE and JENNIFER FADE. CHRISTINE and JENNIFER exit. In semi-darkness, WALTER is sleeping on the sofa, and LENA is lying on the bed UC. Automobile LIGHTS SWEEP across the stage as if beamed into the windows of the house. A car HORN sounds loudly and repeatedly. WALTER sits up. LENA, also, awakens, and both hear what follows. SOUND of two car doors SLAMMING offstage. The HORN sounds again, loudly, once, twice.)

CHRIS (VOICE OFF)
Sh–h–h–h–h! Hush! You'll wake up the whole neighborhood! Sh–h–h–h! Good night. No, don't you dare! Don't honk that horn again!

(SOUND of horn honking, offstage, once more, not very loud.)

You're terrible! Good night.

JENNY (VOICE OFF)
Good night. I had a nice time.

(CHRIS and JENNY enter DL on the porch.)

CHRIS
(Fumbling in HER purse.)
I can't see a thing. Where are my keys?

JENNY
(As if trying the handle of the door.)
The door's unlocked.

(CHRIS and JENNY turn and wave.)

CHRIS and JENNY
Good night.
>(The car LIGHTS withdraw, as the car is HEARD driving away. CHRIS and JENNY enter the kitchen area as if through the back door from the porch.)

CHRIS
Here, let me turn on the light. There.
>(Dim light RISES. JENNY accidentally knocks over a chair.)

Sh–h–h–h! You're as bad as they are!

JENNY
Those crazy boys, honking that horn all the way down Main Street! Did you see the man on the corner? He looked at us as if we were crazy.
>(JENNY imitates the way the man looked. BOTH break down in giggles and try to hush each other.)

JENNY and CHRIS
Sh–h–h–h!

JENNY
>(Whirling around with HER arms outstretched.)

Beer! Wine! Champagne! I want to be alive! I want to be drunk! I want to live!

CHRIS
You are drunk! All that from one beer?

JENNY
I'm drunk on life! I want to live! And dance! And love! And never sleep again!

CHRIS
You must have had a good time. Do you like him?

JENNY
Who?

CHRIS
Who? Paul, of course!

JENNY
Oh, him. He's all right, I guess.

CHRIS
You guess?
    (Ironically.)
Sounds like love at first sight.
    (Eagerly.)
Well, he certainly likes you!

JENNY
He doesn't even know who I am. I'm invisible!

CHRIS
Well, he saw something he liked. He said he liked you very much. Maybe it was love at first sight.

JENNY
I don't care. I'm in love with life and love and poetry and Walt Whitman and the night and the stars!
    (SHE recites with her arms thrown wide.)
  I call to the earth and sea half-held by the night.
  Still nodding night—mad naked summer night.
  Smile, for your lover comes.
  You have given me love—therefore I to you give love!
  Oh unspeakable passionate love!

CHRIS

Wow! That must have been some kiss!

JENNY

I didn't feel anything. I was hoping it would be great! But I didn't feel a thing.

CHRIS

That's because you've never really been kissed.

JENNY

Did you feel passionate when Frank first kissed you?

CHRIS

Not at first, but it gets better as you go along.

JENNY

I hope so. I would hate to think it would always be so—disappointing. I feel all—unsatisfied. Awake! Alive! Longing for—something —that didn't happen. I'll never be able to sleep.

CHRIS

I better not fix you any coffee. You'll never settle down.

JENNY

I don't want to ever settle down. I don't want to know what I'm going to do tomorrow and the next day and the next. When I drive by ordinary, little houses and think that people live all their lives there and never know anything else—how can they stand it?

CHRIS

Some people are happy in their ordinary, little houses.

JENNY

That's all right for you, maybe, but it's not all right for me.

CHRIS
Well, Miss High and Mighty, that's a snooty thing to say.

JENNY
I don't care! I don't want to settle down, ever! Let's never, ever settle down, Chris.

CHRIS
It wouldn't be as bad as you think.

JENNY
You and Frank were down by the lake for a long time. What happened? What? Tell me! Did he ask you to marry him? Is that it?

CHRIS
Maybe.

JENNY
Oh, tell me!

CHRIS
He wants me to marry him when I graduate in June.

JENNY
Oh, Chris! To get married! In June!

CHRIS
I thought you didn't believe in getting married.

JENNY
I don't. But it would be like being in a play. What will we wear?

CHRIS
I haven't said yes yet.

JENNY

Are you going to?

CHRIS

I don't know. Perhaps.

JENNY

Do you love him?

CHRIS

Yes—I think so. At least—he loves me. He's good and kind. He has a good job. I can always depend on him.

JENNY

But do you love him? Or are you thinking of marrying Frank just to get away from all this?

CHRIS

What do you know whether I love Frank? You never loved anyone! All I've ever seen you do is get them to love you, then drop them cold and not care how they feel!

JENNY

I don't ask them to love me. That's their own fault.

CHRIS

It couldn't possibly be your fault, could it? Well, my parents aren't my fault! What about me? Doesn't anyone care what happens to me? I want to live and be alive before I die! Don't I count?

JENNY

I want to live and be alive before I die! But I won't settle for marrying the first one that comes along. And you shouldn't either!

CHRIS

Maybe I shouldn't marry anyone! Maybe I'll get to be as crazy as she is. Maybe one day I'll walk the house like a zombie and set fire to everything and let it burn!

        (CHRIS turns away with a stifled sob. JENNY quickly goes to CHRIS and puts HER arms around CHRIS.)

JENNY
Oh, Chris, I'm sorry! It will be all right. It will be all right.

CHRIS
How do people get that way, Jenny? How do they get that way? That's what I'm afraid of. He said he loved her once. He said she was the prettiest girl he ever saw. Now look at them! Can you imagine them ever being in love?

JENNY
I don't know, Chris.

CHRIS
Will we just grow old and crazy and drunk to shut out the pain and all the poetry forgotten and all the dreams?

JENNY
Oh, Chris, we can't grow old or forget our dreams or die. That won't happen to us.

CHRIS
All I know, if I stay here I'll be dying every day, and one day I'll be old and crazy and dead.

JENNY
Don't stay here! You can go away! You can! I'm going to go away when I'm old enough and never come back. You can go away!

CHRIS
Can you go away from being crazy?

JENNY
You'll never be crazy. You're the sanest person I know, and the smartest, and the best!

CHRIS
That's easy for you to say.

JENNY
That's the hardest thing for me to say – calling somebody else the smartest and the best!

CHRIS
Oh, you! How did I get a friend like you?

JENNY
Just lucky, I guess. Are you feeling better now?
    (CHRIS nods.)
Hey! What time is it! I've got to get home. My father will be furious! Good night, ladies, good night, sweet ladies, good night, good night.

CHRIS
Good night, Sweet Prince, and flights of angels guide thee to thy rest.

    (JENNY exits by the DL door. CHRIS waves goodbye. SPOT on JENNIFER DL.)

JENNIFER
    (Calling after JENNY.)
Jenny! Jenny!

CHRISTINE
It does no good calling. She can't hear you.

JENNIFER
But I want to tell her. It's never as we thought it would be.

CHRISTINE
You can't tell her. She hasn't lived it yet.

JENNIFER
Mrs. Kraus! You were listening. Christine is here. Speak to her.

LENA
>(Standing.)

Christine is dead. We are all dead.

JENNIFER
No! She's still alive! Speak to her.
>(LENA stares into the dark. After a moment, JENNIFER calls to WALTER.)

Mr. Kraus! Christine is here. Go to her. She loves you. Speak to her.

WALTER
>(Slowly rising and crossing into the kitchen area.)

Christine.

CHRIS
I thought you were asleep. Did we wake you?

WALTER
No. I wasn't sleeping.

CHRIS
Did you hear what we said?

WALTER
>(As HE sinks dejectedly into a chair.)

Yes, I heard.... Chris! You're all I have!

CHRIS

Don't you see? I've got to have a life of my own!

WALTER

You're all I have, Chris. You're all I have! What will I do if you leave me now? What will I do—without you?

CHRIS

I'm not going to spend the rest of my life living in this house and looking after both of you! Don't I have a life to live! Don't I count?
(Pause.)
There's no privacy in this house! I feel trapped! Trapped! I'm going to get away from here! I can't stand it any longer! I'm going to marry Frank and get away from here!

WALTER

We need you, Christine! I need you!

CHRIS
(Angrily approaching HIM.)
I don't care! I didn't ask to be born! It's not my fault! It's not fair!

WALTER
(Grabbing at CHRIS, and managing to pin HER.)
Don't go away!

CHRIS
(As SHE struggles to escape from HIS desperate clutch.)
No...! Don't...! Stop it!

(SHE manages to break free.)

WALTER

Don't leave me! You're all I have!

CHRIS
Stay away from me! I hate you! I hate this house! I hate everything! You disgusting drunk!

(CHRIS exits into the hall L, as WALTER stares after her.)

WALTER
(Almost to HIMSELF.)
Christine...! Oh, Christine...!

(LIGHTS dim on the main set. SPOT on JENNIFER DL. In the distortion of JENNIFER'S dream, WALTER now takes on the persona of JENNIFER'S FATHER.)

JENNIFER
Daddy...! Daddy!

WALTER as JENNIFER'S FATHER
(Standing and turning toward JENNIFER. His stance has become firm, self-assured, and HE speaks in a new, authoritative voice.)
Jenny! You never listen to a thing I say!

JENNIFER
Oh, Daddy, you wouldn't come to my wedding, or let my mother come!

WALTER as JENNIFER'S FATHER
You must not marry this boy. You don't love him.

JENNIFER
I will marry him! I'll not let you tell me what to do!

WALTER as JENNIFER'S FATHER
It will be the biggest mistake of your life!

JENNIFER
I won't know that until I've lived the rest of my life!
    (Pause.)
Don't you see? I've got to make my own mistakes! You can't make my mistakes for me!

WALTER as JENNIFER'S FATHER
If you'll break this engagement, I'll send you to Europe. You can go anywhere you want. I'll pay the bills.

JENNIFER
Oh, Daddy, what have you done? What have you done? This boy Paul is a stranger to me—but you have said the one thing what will force me to marry him! I'd rather destroy us both than be bought and sold! Can't you see that? Can't you see?
    (WALTER as JENNIFER'S FATHER slowly turns away.)
I'll not let you tell me what to do! All my life, I'll not let anyone tell me what to do!

    (DL LIGHTS FADE. WALTER, now again in the persona of CHRIS'S FATHER, sits, resuming his despondent attitude. CHRISTINE enters DL, where SHE stands watching the following stage action. JENNIFER rises, and stands opposite CHRISTINE, also watching the stage action. WALTER regresses to a younger self.)

WALTER
(Stands, eagerly calling.)
Len...! Len!

(WALTER picks up an imaginary pebble and seems to toss it at a window. LENA moves toward WALTER from the upstage bedroom. She, too, seems much younger and now evidences the grace of youth.)

LENA

Is that you, Walt?

WALTER

Over here! Come on out!

LENA

(Crossing to join WALTER.)
Oh, Walt! Sh–h–h–h! They might hear us!

WALTER

I want them to know. I want the world to know how much I love you!

LENA

Walt! If they hear us....

WALTER

(Drawing HER into HIS arms.)
Oh, Len, I've missed you. I've longed for you. You're like the moon—shining and mysterious and far away. Oh, Len, I want you. Feel how I want you!

LENA

Oh, Walt, if my father finds out, he'll kill me. You don't know what he's like when he's angry.

WALTER

I don't care if he finds out. All I know is I want you. All I could think of was the night when we were lying in the meadow and the night was all around us and we were turning with the stars.

LENA

Yes, we were turning with the stars. And your face was dark and strange above mine—a darker night against the dark. Oh, Walt, I long for you. I don't care if he finds out.

WALTER

I don't want you to ever leave me. Come—I want you now!

(WALTER takes LENA'S hand, and they exit R.)

JENNIFER

You told me he loved her when they first met. Oh, Christine, did he really love her that much? Did it really happen like that?

CHRISTINE

Only in your dream—where all of us live again.

(LIGHTS FADE on CHRISTINE and JENNIFER.)

END OF SCENE TWO

ACT I: SCENE THREE

(JENNIFER is in HER area DL, observing the scene which follows. DORINE and LENA are in the Living Room.)

DORINE
Sit down, Lena. The taxi be here in a few minutes.

LENA
Dorine, don't tell anybody. They took my pills.

DORINE
Who took your pills, honey?

LENA
Dorine, I'm afraid.

DORINE
What you afraid of?

LENA
Those men....

DORINE
What men, honey?

LENA
Those men—hiding in my room. They took my pills.

DORINE
They ain't no men takin' your pills, Lena. You just—dreamin' 'bout those men.

LENA
No men—hiding? They call me when I try to sleep. They hide in the closet. Sometimes they laugh at me.

DORINE

Now don't you pay them no never mind. Dorine is goin' to take a broom and chase them outta the house if they don't leave you alone. You tell them now, you hear? They better leave you alone or Dorine goin' to fix their wagon.

LENA

Dorine, don't leave me.

DORINE

Don't you worry, honey. Dorine is here. I won't let nothin' hurt you.

LENA

You are kind to me, Dorine. You are a kind woman.

DORINE

What kinda world we got, if we cain't be kind to each other? Lord, in this world, we got to be kind to each other!

> (CHRIS enters from the hall L, holding a book which she is studying intently. SHE ignores DORINE and LENA as SHE paces, studying.)

JENNIFER
(DL.)

Mrs. Kraus! Mrs. Kraus, it's me—Jenny! I'm here and Chris is here. Speak to her. Tell Chris that you're afraid!

LENA
(Not looking at JENNIFER.)

She wouldn't understand.

DORINE

Who wouldn't understand?

LENA

Christine wouldn't understand. She's dead.

DORINE
No, she ain't, Lena. She's right here.

JENNIFER
She's here with you. She's alive. Speak to her.

LENA
No, no one understands. Christine is dead. We are all dead.

CHRIS
Oh, Mother, for God's sake! I'm trying to study! You're the one who's dead! Wake up! Wake up!

DORINE
Sh–h–h–h–h now. It's all right. I'll see if the taxi come.

>(SHE exits into the shop R. JENNY enters DR. LENA turns to the window.)

JENNY
Hello, Miz Kraus.
>(LENA does not answer.)

Chris, are you home?

CHRIS
Come on in.

JENNY
I've got to drive over to Maple Avenue and run an errand for my father. Come with me.

CHRIS
I can't. Dorine has to take mother to the doctor. Daddy may need me in the shop.

JENNY
What are you doing?

CHRIS
Studying my catechism. I'm supposed to go over it with Father Joseph.

JENNY
Are you really going to become a Catholic?

CHRIS
I'll have to if I'm going to marry Frank.

JENNY
But how can it be something you have to learn from a book? Like studying French. I just don't understand that. It doesn't make any sense.

CHRIS
Well, I've got to memorize all this whether it makes any sense or not.

JENNY
Or even whether you believe it?

CHRIS
I believe in marrying Frank! That's what I believe in! Now do you understand?

JENNY
No, I don't!

(SHE turns away angrily. DORINE and WALTER enter from shop R.)

DORINE
Come on, Lena. The taxi's here. We better go on.

WALTER
You better get on out there. I guess I pay enough already. Don't need to keep him waiting.

(DORINE starts to lead LENA through shop door R.)

LENA
(Hesitates.)
Are the men out there?

DORINE
If any those men mess with you, I'm goin' to punch them in the nose. Let's go.
(LENA hesitates.)
It's all right. Dorine's with you. Ain't no men goin' to get by me.

(DORINE leads LENA. THEY exit R.)

WALTER
(To CHRIS.)
You better come on in the shop. With Dorine gone I'm going to need your help.

CHRIS
You can call me if you get busy. I have to study my catechism.

WALTER
(Sarcastically.)
Study your catechism!

CHRIS
Yes. I'm supposed to see Father Joseph this afternoon.

WALTER
(Sarcastically.)
Father Joseph! We never had any Catholics in our family, and we don't need any now.

CHRIS
We never had anything in our family!

WALTER

Our family was all Church of God people far back as I can remember.

CHRIS

When did I ever have a family? When did we ever go to church?

WALTER

Well, it wouldn't be a Catholic one, that's for sure! And don't ask me to kneel and such as that at your wedding 'cause I won't do it!

CHRIS

When did I ever ask you to do anything?

WALTER

Well, I'm paying for everything, I guess. But I won't kneel!

CHRIS

Oh, leave me alone! Just leave me alone!
    (WALTER exits into the shop R.)
Oh, it's all going to be ruined! The whole wedding! With him drunk and her crazy! Oh, it's all going to be ruined!

JENNY

It's going to be all right. I'll be there with you. I won't let anything ruin your wedding day! You'll see! We've always shared everything together. Think of all the things we've shared that no one else could share with us.
    (Trying to divert Chris' pessimistic thoughts.)
Do you remember when you used to go to piano lessons with me and we'd ride our bicycles on out into the country and just forget about piano lessons? We should be geniuses by now; we've had so many lessons.

CHRIS

Do you remember Miss Caraway?

                        JENNY
And the painting lessons!

                        CHRIS
In that big house with the pillars.

                        JENNY
And only three of the downstairs room were furnished. All the other rooms were empty and echoed when we walked.

                        CHRIS
And the studio was upstairs.

                        JENNY
And we'd walk through the echoing hall, calling to each other—"Hello."

                        CHRIS
"Hello."

                        JENNY
"Is anyone there?"

                        CHRIS
"Anyone there…?" Do you remember, Miss Caraway was stone deaf and had to read our lips?

            (LIGHTS slowly FADE to a soft GLOW.)

                        JENNY
We're upstairs in the studio. You are sitting at the easel.
            (CHRIS moves slowly upstage of JENNY and
            stands, her back to the audience, as if painting at
            an easel.)
There is a big mirror in a gilt frame over the mantel. You are painting—the red roses in a cut glass vase on the table, their scent filling the air, mingling with the sharp smell of paint and turpentine and dust and the heat of summer.

CHRIS
"You're so restless, Jenny. Why don't you paint something?"

JENNY
"I don't want to." And because I am bored, I make a face at Miss Caraway behind her back, and I say, "Hello, is anyone there?"

CHRIS
"Anyone there?"

JENNY
And I say something mean and childish behind Miss Caraway's back because I am bored. "I bet she never had a sweetheart in her life. How can she live like this, alone, and no one caring? It must be terrible to be deaf and dumb! She doesn't know anything!" And suddenly, as if a thin curtain had parted, I look up at the mirror over the mantelpiece.
>(JENNY crosses DL. Light RISES to DIM on JEN-
>NIFER. JENNY and JENNIFER stand facing each
>other.)

And you are mirrored there. And I look into Miss Caraway's eyes in the mirror, and I know that she has been reading our lips all along—that she has always been able to read our lips in the mirror when we thought she couldn't see us.
>(JENNY moves HER hand as if touching the mir-
>ror with blind eyes.)

And I had the strangest feeling, as if there were two young girls...

JENNIFER and JENNY
...and two women looking at each other in the mirror.
>(JENNIFER, also, moves her hand, a few inches
>from JENNY'S hand, mirroring JENNY'S move-
>ments.)

And I see the look in Miss Caraway's eyes and I want to say, "I'm sorry."

JENNIFER
"How can she live like this, alone, and no one caring?" And I know now what she had always known.

> (CHRIS and JENNY cross to table and sit. SPOT remains on JENNIFER.)

The house silent and lonely when the echoes die away. Is anyone there? Anyone there? Oh, Jordan, where are you? Where are you? I never loved anyone before you. Not my husband, Paul, not anyone. I was afraid of loving and being loved. I've looked into the mirror of their eyes, finding my reflection, searching for that feeling I never had. But when I looked into your eyes, there was no space between us anymore. Oh, Jordan, where are you?

> (SPOT FADES on JENNIFER. JENNIFER exits. LIGHTS RISE on main set.)

CHRIS
Jenny? Jenny! You look so far away. Wake up!

JENNY
I was just thinking about Miss Caraway. And the house, silent and lonely when the echoes died away. And the sad and lonely look in her eyes. I was so ashamed of what I had said behind her back.

CHRIS
I've never before heard you say you were ashamed of anything. Sometimes you are so into yourself. You get that faraway look.

JENNY
I have a feeling about things, but I just can't put it into words. I feel restless and impatient! There's a dream I have that I do the same things over and over and I can't stop and I'm tired and bored and I just want to break something, anything, just to feel that something is happening and that I'm alive.

CHRIS
You'll be going off to college when you graduate and then you'll get a job and get married.

JENNY
But what does all that mean? I don't want to get a job! I would hate it! I can't do anything the world thinks is important.

CHRIS
You'll get married and then you won't have to do anything important.

JENNY
That's a depressing thing to say.

CHRIS
But it's true. I know you better than you know yourself. You'll get married like everyone else. I think Paul is in love with you.

JENNY
Well, I'm not in love with him. I'm not going out with him again.

CHRIS
What do you mean you're not going out with him? You know he and Frank are coming down from Louisville tomorrow night, and you said you'd go dancing with us.

JENNY
I don't care. I don't want to go out with him.

CHRIS
But what will you tell him?

JENNY
I won't tell him anything. I'm not going to see him again.

CHRIS

When did you decide that?

JENNY

Just now.

CHRIS

But you can't do that! How would he feel?

JENNY

I don't care how he feels. I didn't ask him to love me.

CHRIS

Just go out with him this once and then you don't have to see him again.

JENNY

No, I don't want to.

CHRIS

You don't want to? You don't want to! And you think that decides everything! You are spoiled and selfish!

JENNY

It's dishonest to pretend to believe something you don't believe! To read your feelings from a catechism! I don't want to ever pretend to feel anything unless I feel it with my whole heart!

CHRIS

"I—I—I !" Can't you ever think about anyone else but yourself for a change! Why don't you grow up!

JENNY

What's so great about growing up! The grown-ups I know spend their lives doing such stupid, useless things! Washing pots and pans and saying the same things over and over and never saying what they really mean!

CHRIS
Washing pots and pans? You never washed anything in your life! You think you're so special! Well, you're just like everyone else! You pretend! You're not really Cyrano when you act the part. That's pretending! My noble love! My shining dream! My great poetry! What great poetry have you ever written?

JENNY
That's not pretending! Don't you know anything about Truth and Beauty and Poetry more than pots and pans and catechisms! "Beauty is Truth and Truth Beauty! That is all ye know on earth and all ye need to know!" And I thought you believed it, too!

(BOTH are silent for a long moment.)

CHRIS
Oh, Jenny, I don't know what to believe. I just want to try to be happy. I'm not sure I can.

JENNY
  (Impulsively, JENNY crosses to CHRIS and hugs her.)
Chris, I'm sorry. You will be happy! I know it! Let's not get mad at each other.

CHRIS
Will you still be my maid of honor at the wedding even if I do become a Catholic?

JENNY
You know I will. I want you to be happy more than anything.
  (Looking at her watch.)
Look at the time. I've got to go.

(SHE starts to exit.)

CHRIS

But what will I tell Paul?

JENNY

You'll think of something. You always do.

CHRIS

Jenny, wait. I don't know what to tell him.

JENNY
(Walking backward as SHE talks.)
Consult your catechism, Chris. It has all the answers. See you at your wedding.

(JENNY waves goodbye.)

CHRIS
(Half laughing, half serious.)
You're absolutely impossible!

JENNY

I know. That's why I'm so lovable!

(SHE waves again and then exits by the porch.)

CHRIS
(Calling after HER.)
I won't tell him, Jenny. Do you hear? You'll have to tell him!

(Light FADES on CHRIS. SHE exits. LIGHTS RISE at DR and DL. JENNY enters DR, and JENNIFER and JORDAN enter DL.)

JENNY
(As if speaking to her husband, Paul.)
Paul, what is it? What's wrong? Tell me what you're thinking.

JENNIFER
Oh, Jordan, how could everything go so wrong? I thought no one could ever know me as you did.

JORDAN
I do know you, every part of you, every curve of you, and you know me.

JENNIFER
No, I don't know you!

JENNY
You lied to me!

JORDAN
What do you mean?

JENNIFER
What do I mean? You aren't divorced! You were never divorced! You lied to me!

JORDAN
Jenny, I've never loved anyone as I love you. I've never been as close to anyone.

JENNIFER
What about your wife? Did you say that when you were fucking her?

JORDAN
She and I haven't slept in the same bed in years.

JENNY
Another lie!

JENNIFER
To go with all your other lies!

JORDAN
You love me! Say it!

JENNIFER and JENNY
Oh, leave me alone!

JORDAN
Say it! Say it!

JENNIFER
I do love you. I love you with all my heart. I can't stop loving you even when I know you lied to me.

JENNY
I feel lost.

JORDAN
Listen to me! I didn't plan that you'd walk into the Players Club that night. I didn't plan that we'd fall in love. It just happened. You can't control life.

JENNIFER
Control! My world is falling apart.

JENNY
Don't lie to me anymore, Paul. Where were you?

JENNIFER
When we met, you said you were divorced. I believed you!

JORDAN
It isn't as simple as you think.

JENNY
Paul, you were with someone else, weren't you

JENNIFER
Why did you lie to me?

JORDAN

You know why. If I told you the truth that night when we met, that I was still married, would you have stayed with me?

JENNIFER

(Hesitating.)

I don't know.

JORDAN

That's your answer. I couldn't take the chance of losing you.

JENNIFER

I trusted you!

JENNY

Not to leave me when I needed you.

JENNIFER

Not to lie to me when I needed you. When you were away those long months, without caring how I felt, did you think I would just sit on a shelf waiting for you to come back?

JENNY

Where were you?

JENNIFER

Just tell me the truth!

JORDAN

Do you really want the truth? You don't need me. You want me and I want you, but you don't need me. My wife has been ill for a long time. She panics when she has to go out. She can function as long as she knows I'll come back. We have two sons. You know that. I couldn't leave them when they needed me. I can't leave them now. That's the truth.

JENNIFER
I see. Now I'm going to tell you the truth. See if you can stand it.

JENNY
No more lies between us anymore.

JENNIFER
When you were away those long months, I had an affair with someone else.

JORDAN
(Reacting as if stunned.)
You—you were with someone else?
(HE grabs HER by the shoulders.)
You were in his arms! You let him touch you—the way I touch you!

JENNIFER
No one can touch me the way you touch me.

JORDAN
Liar!

JENNY
I promised to be faithful! I kept my promise!

JORDAN
Faithful?

JENNIFER
What promise have you kept?

JORDAN
My God, Jenny, why did you do it?

JENNIFER
Why did I do it? Do you think there's a simple answer. It was something I had to do—to break your spell over me.

JENNY
I was at home with my parents...

JENNIFER
...and then I was married to Paul. And then I met you. I thought we were meant to be together. Then I found out that you lied to me.

JORDAN
And you've lied to me.

JENNIFER
Yes.... I didn't know who I was anymore.

JENNY
Where is the woman I thought I would be?

JENNIFER
Don't you see? If I only live in the mirror of men's eyes...

JENNY
...As if gazing into a dark pool....

JENNIFER
I could do that—go down into that dark pool. But I would have to give up something in myself I value—some quiet place. I had to choose. Just as you had to choose.

(JENNY starts to exit.)

JORDAN
Jenny, don't leave me! I need you.

JENNIFER
No, she needs you. You said it yourself.

JORDAN
Jenny...!

JENNIFER

It's all right. I understand more than you know. I'll never love anyone as I love you. I'll never want anyone as I want you. I only know that I've got to get away from you for now.

JENNY

For now....

JENNIFER

To put some distance between us...

JENNY

...to find out who I am.

(JENNY exits.)

JORDAN

Jenny...!

JENNIFER

Don't follow me. Just—let me go.

(JENNIFER exits.)

JORDAN

Jenny! Jenny!

SLOW FADE to BLACKOUT

END OF SCENE THREE

END OF ACT ONE

ACT II: SCENE ONE

(SPOT on JENNIFER DL.)

JENNIFER
In my darkest hour I dream in vivid color
Of a Happy Place full of laughter and dancing and joy.
And I know that within me is a happy place that I must find again,
Full of laughter and dancing and joy.

(SPOT on JENNIFER FADES. JENNIFER exits. Lighting on main set becomes that of a BRIGHT June morning. It is Chris's wedding day. LENA is sitting at the kitchen table, where CHRIS is standing, a comb in HER hand, arranging LENA'S hair. A hand mirror and bobby pins are on the table. LENA wears a becoming dress, stockings, dress shoes with medium heels. CHRIS is in a white satin slip with lace trim, white high-heeled shoes, and sheer hose.)

CHRIS
Now look at me, Mother.

LENA
(Looking up like an obedient child.)
You're fixing my hair. Is it our wedding day?

CHRIS
It's my wedding day.

LENA
That's why you're fixing my hair?

CHRIS
This doesn't want to stay put. Let me see—there.

WALTER
(Entering from hall at L.)
Christine, where is my shaving soap?

(WALTER is in a sleeveless undershirt and dark "Sunday" trousers worn with suspenders.)

CHRIS
Did you take a bath yet?

WALTER
You heard the water running, didn't you?

CHRIS
That doesn't mean anything.

WALTER
I guess I know how to take a bath. I don't need you telling me how. Where's my shaving soap?

CHRIS
It's right there.

WALTER
(Exits L, VOICE OFF.)
Well, I don't see it! It's not here!

CHRIS
Yes, it is.

WALTER (VOICE OFF)
Well, I can't find it.

CHRIS
For heaven's sake! It's right in front of your eyes!
(SHE slams the comb down on the table and exits into the hall L. VOICE OFF.)

You can't find anything!
>(WALTER enters and stands peevishly. CHRIS enters, handing him the shaving soap.)

Didn't I tell you? It was right in front of your eyes.

WALTER

That's not the kind I use.

CHRIS

That's all they had, so you'll just have to use it.

WALTER

Then I'm not going to shave. I shaved yesterday.

CHRIS

You didn't have any soap yesterday! Now you go on and shave. I don't want to hear another word out of you about it. You are not going to my wedding with your beard all scraggly. You just go on now, do you hear?

WALTER
>(Exiting into the hall L.)

Well, I don't need you to tell me when to shave.

CHRIS
>(Holding the mirror where LENA can see her image.)

Now, see how you look.
>(LENA'S expression of child-like compliance not changing, SHE starts to reach up to touch HER hair.)

No, don't you touch it. You keep your hands down now and don't you touch it. It looks fine just that way, and don't you mess it up.
>(Calling.)

Daddy, will you hurry up in there!

WALTER
>(Entering from hall at L.)

Well, what do you want me to do? Shave or hurry up?

CHRIS
(Exasperated.)
Oh!

(WALTER shrugs and exits L. DORINE enters from porch DR. She is carrying a stack of flower boxes. DORINE is as dressed up as can be with a flowered hat, flowered dress, white shoes and gloves, and a large white pocketbook.)

DORINE
My, if it ain't a pretty day! You all decent?

CHRIS
Is that you, Dorine?

DORINE
It sure is, if you can find me behind all these here flower boxes. I never seed so many corsages.
(CHRIS helps DORINE put the flower boxes on the table.)
Honey, you goin' to have the sun smile on you today!

(DORINE hugs CHRIS, and CHRIS hugs DORINE warmly. CHRIS opens the biggest box and takes out a large bouquet of pink and white sweetheart roses.)

CHRIS
Oh, they're beautiful!
(CHRIS smells the roses and then opens one of the small boxes. She removes a corsage and holds it up to DORINE'S shoulder.)
Doesn't that look pretty on your new dress? My, my, you're so dressed up!

DORINE
I got to look nice for my baby's wedding.
(Smelling the corsage before SHE pins it on.)
M–m–m–m! That do smell good!

WALTER
(Entering from the hall L.)
How much did all those flowers cost?

CHRIS
Don't worry. You didn't have to pay for them.

WALTER
Well, I had to pay for everything else.

CHRIS
(Handing one of the corsages to DORINE.)
Here's Mother's corsage. Will you put it on her? I've got to get dressed.

DORINE
I sure will.

CHRIS
And don't let her touch her hair. I just fixed it.

(CHRIS exits into the hall L.)

DORINE
(To LENA.)
My, don't you look pretty. Lena, you look real pretty.

LENA
Do I?

DORINE
Did Christine fix your hair. Why, she done the same as a beautician.

(LENA starts to raise her hand to touch her hair, and DORINE gently stops her.)

No, now, don't you touch it, Honey. You look real pretty. Lemme just put on this here corsage and then we goin' to go on in and finish getting' dressed.

(DORINE pins the corsage on LENA'S dress. WALTER enters from the hall L.)

Don't Lena look real pretty, Walter?

WALTER

(Crossing to the living room, muttering, and taking care not to look at Lena.)

If you call an old buzzard "pretty."

DORINE

Now, don't you say that, Walter. She looks real pretty.

(DORINE speaks in the direction of the departing WALTER, but only loud enough for LENA to hear.)

Don't you listen to him. He don't know nothin'. He just grouchy. And we know why. Don't we, Honey? We know why he so grouchy. Men! They ain't no account!

(In the living room, WALTER finds a pint bottle of whiskey hidden behind the sofa. HE sits on the sofa, brooding and muttering to himself and taking swigs from the bottle. DORINE takes LENA gently by the arm.)

Come on now, Lena. We goin' to go in and finish gettin' dressed.

LENA

(As THEY cross to upstage bedroom.)

Christine bought me a new dress.

DORINE

Yes, I know, honey, and it's mighty pretty. We goin' to put on some of this here rose sachet I bought and, my, don't we smell good!

(THEY enter the upstage bedroom where LENA sits on the bed. JENNY enters by the porch DL. JENNY, now 16 years old, is wearing white high heels, stockings, and a sleeveless, princess style dress. She is carrying a straw bonnet with flowers on it, white gloves, a small, white purse, and a small book bound in blue velvet.)

JENNY
Hi, Chris. Am I too early?

CHRIS (VOICE OFF)
Oh, Jenny, I need you. I'm never going to get ready on time.

JENNY
Yes, you will.
(Calling into the upstage bedroom.)
Hello, Miz Kraus. Hi, Dorine. It's a beautiful day!

DORINE
It sure is.

(CHRIS enters from the hall L.)

JENNY
Chris, it's a beautiful day! Happy the bride the sun shines on! Happy wedding day, Chris!

(THEY hug each other.)

CHRIS
Oh, don't mess my hair.

JENNY
Is that what you're going to say to Frank tonight?

CHRIS

Oh, you...!

JENNY
(As SHE admires CHRIS.)

What a sexy slip!

CHRIS

Do you like it?

JENNY

Wow! Do I! Look—I'm pretty sexy, too.

(SHE displays the edge of her slip, which is edged in lace.)

CHRIS

We're both sexy!

JENNY

Is that what you're going to say to Frank tonight?

CHRIS

You are terrible!

JENNY

Here....

(JENNY hands CHRIS a slim volume of poetry bound in blue velvet with the word "POEMS" inexpertly embroidered on the cover. CHRIS examines the book.)

It's our favorite poems. I wrote them out and bound them myself, in velvet.

CHRIS

What's this on the cover? "P—U ?"

JENNY
It's not P—U! I tried to embroider the word "Poems" on the cover, but you can't read it very well.

CHRIS
(Opening the book.)
Without, the frost, the blinding snow,
The storm-wind's moody madness –
Within, the firelight's ruddy glow,
And childhood's nest of gladness.
The magic words shall hold thee fast:
Thou shalt not heed the raving blast.
It's beautiful.

JENNY
Something to remember me by.

CHRIS
But you'll come to visit us. Louisville is only ninety miles away.

JENNY
Yes, but it won't be the same. I feel it. But that's okay. That's the way it's supposed to be.
(SHE strikes a pose.)
One day you'll be with your husband and your ten little children....

CHRIS
Ten children!

JENNY
(Acting in an exaggerated manner.)
And you'll say, "I wonder what ever became of Jenny?" And at that very moment, I'll be regretting my wild and depraved and decadent life, drinking absinthe and dancing the tango with my latest lover in low dive in Paris!

(JENNY dances a tango step which culminates in a tragic pose.)

CHRIS
Dancing the tango and drinking absinthe! You mad, impetuous fool!

JENNY
Ah, where are the snows of yesteryear?

CHRIS
What a wonderful gift! We'll read it on our honeymoon. And you will come back from Paris to visit us.

JENNY
Oh your honeymoon? That is French!

CHRIS
No, don't you dare! You are terrible!

JENNY
I know. Isn't it fun! Now let me see your nightgown.

CHRIS
I'll get it.

(SHE exits into the hall L then returns, holding up a bridal nightgown in white and lace.)

JENNY
You can see right through it!

(SHE takes the nightgown and holds it in front of HER body.)

CHRIS
Hey, I've got to get dressed. It's getting late.

(CHRIS exits into the hall. JENNY continues to hold the nightgown before HER and dances with it. WALTER, tipsy but not drunk, rises from the sofa and sees JENNY waltzing to the music.)

WALTER

Jenny, we're going to dance at my wedding!

(WALTER, lightly, takes JENNY into HIS arms and leads HER in a whirling dance. JENNY drops the nightgown over a chair. HE is surprisingly graceful as they dance.)

JENNY

You're a really good dancer, Mr. Kraus.

WALTER

I used to be a champion ballroom dancer.

JENNY

Did you ever win any prizes?

WALTER

Only the prize for being a good kisser.

JENNY

Oh, Mr. Kraus!

DORINE

(Crossing from the upstage bedroom to join in the fun.)

Now what kind o' foolin' goin' on out here?

WALTER

We're not foolin', are we, Jenny? This is real dancing! They don't dance like this anymore!

DORINE

Praise the Lord!

WALTER

Dorine, come on! We're going to show 'em how!

DORINE

You the limit! You all roused up.

(WALTER takes DORINE in HIS arms and whirls HER around. CHRIS enters from the hall R. SHE is dressed in her wedding dress, a white princess style dress, and is carrying a white satin hat with a short veil.)

CHRIS

Daddy, what are you doing?

WALTER

We're dancing at my wedding. Right, Jenny? Right, Dorine?

CHRIS

You're not even dressed yet!

WALTER

I guess I can dance at my own wedding!

CHRIS
(Laughing, not scolding.)
Daddy, stop that and get dressed!

WALTER

I'm dancing!

CHRIS
(Now with concern.)
Daddy! If you don't get dressed right now, we're all going to be late for my wedding!

DORINE
(Cautioning, not scolding.)
Walter, you better get youself dressed!

(WALTER notices the nightgown draped over the chair. He picks up the nightgown and holds it before him as he dances alone in a silly manner, wiggling his hips and speaking in a high voice as if he is a bride.)

WALTER
Oh, ain't I pretty! You can see my tits!

CHRIS
(Not able to keep from laughing.)
Oh, Daddy, stop that!

(CHRIS tries to snatch the nightgown away, but WALTER eludes her.)

WALTER
(Now across the room from CHRIS and flourishing the nightgown.)
This nightgown is no good for a bride!

CHRIS
What do you mean it's no good for a bride?

WALTER
It doesn't have fur on the bottom.

CHRIS
(Innocently taking the bait.)
Why would a bride want fur on the bottom of her nightgown?

WALTER
To keep her neck warm!

CHRIS
(Embarrassed.)
Oh, Daddy!

(SHE manages to grab the nightgown away from HIM.)

WALTER
Right, Jenny?

JENNY
Right, Mr. Kraus.

WALTER
Right, Dorine? You need fur on the bottom....

DORINE
You goin' to have a switch on you bottom if you don't get youself dressed!

CHRIS
Daddy, stop it! Have you been drinking?

(Sniffing, SHE approaches WALTER.)

WALTER
It's my aftershave lotion.

CHRIS
If it is, you've been drinking it!
(CHRIS begins to cross to the living room.)
You are not going to get sloppy drunk and ruin my wedding day! Now, where is that bottle?
(CHRIS is searching in the living room.)
Dorine, did you see that bottle?

DORINE

I ain't studyin' no bottle!

>(CHRIS locates the bottle in a corner of the sofa, and immediately crosses to the kitchen with the bottle.)

WALTER

Christine! No! Christine!

>(Ignoring WALTER'S protests, CHRIS pours the bottle's contents into the sink.)

DORINE

She know how to slow you down, Walter. You outta whiskey just like a automobile outta gas.

WALTER

What do you know? Didn't I pay for everything? I guess a man can have a drink at his own wedding and dance when he wants to!

JENNY

Happy wedding day, Chris!

CHRIS

>(Laughing.)

You're all crazy! Dorine, get some coffee down him and get him dressed. He can't go to the church like this! Jenny, will you help me? The whole crazy bunch of us will be late!

JENNY

>(Exiting with CHRIS into the hall L.)

All of us will just dance right into the church!

DORINE

Come on, Walter. You party done pooped!

WALTER

I should've won the prize for ballroom dancing.

DORINE

If you don't come in here and finish gettin' dressed', you daughter goin' to give you a prize!

(DORINE starts to exit into the hall L, WALTER following.)

WALTER

(Singing.)
Here comes the bride.
Here comes the groom.
Here comes her father,
Stiff as a broom!

(DORINE and WALTER exit. LENA, now alone, stands, and with a shy, slight smile on HER face, begins a slow, awkward, and yet not graceless dance. The VOICES of CHRIS and JENNY returning is heard offstage. Upon hearing the voices, LENA abruptly stops dancing and returns to sit on the bed upstage. CHRIS and JENNY enter from hall L.)

JENNY

Let me see. Oh, you look beautiful! You're a beautiful bride!

CHRIS

I'm beautiful! And you're beautiful!

JENNY

And we're all beautiful!

CHRIS

(SHE takes her bouquet and a corsage from the icebox and holds it.)

Oh, Jenny, I think we're all crazy, but just for one day, I want to be happy? That's not too much to ask—just for one day.

JENNY

And so shall it be, oh damsel fair.
For this one day I grant your prayer.
And all who heard should see them there,
And all should cry, Beware! Beware!
Her flashing eyes
Her floating hair!
Weave a circle round her thrice,
And close your eyes with holy dread,

JENNY and CHRIS

For she on honey-dew hath fed,
And drunk the milk of paradise.

(LIGHTS dims on CHRIS. JENNY moves downstage, SPOT on HER.)

JENNY

Who is this stranger standing beside me? Why am I marrying Paul who is a stranger to me? I am invisible to him. He does not know the secret of my name—that it will change and I will change and nothing will stay the same.
(As if to Paul)
Oh, Paul, don't say yes! Run now before it's too late! Run away and save us both. You'll run one day and never stop. Run now before it's too late.
(Light on JENNY DIMS.)
Yes, kiss me now, Paul. We're alone. Hold me. Hold me—tighter. Love me, then maybe it will be all right. Hold me. It's all right. It's all right. Don't worry. It's all right. It happens like that sometime, I think. It's all right. Tomorrow will be better. Tomorrow or next week or next year. Sleep now, Paul. It will be all right. Go to sleep now.
(Pause, turning away.)

It is night. Paul is sleeping by my side.
I float out from a dark shore, sailing a darker sea,
The moon is beating a rhythm in my blood
As I lie drowning in the restless tide.

   (SPOT on JENNY FADES as light UP on main set.)

      CHRIS

Jenny, we're going to be late!
   (Calling.)
Daddy, get your jacket on! Dorine, do you have Mother's hat and gloves?

      DORINE

I'll get them.

   (DORINE starts to cross to the upstage bedroom.)

      CHRIS

Jenny, put on your corsage.

   (JENNY pins her corsage to her dress as DORINE stops to admire CHRIS.)

      DORINE

You is the prettiest bride I ever did see!

      CHRIS

Am I? Am I really?

   (DORINE hugs CHRIS and then crosses to the upstage bedroom.)

      JENNY

Just beautiful! How do I look?

CHRIS

Just perfect. Don't change a thing.

(WALTER enters the kitchen. He is dressed very neatly and presentably in a suit and tie. CHRIS looks him over, turning him around. She adjusts his tie.)

Daddy, you look very handsome. Wait....

(CHRIS puts HER bouquet on the table and takes out a red carnation from one of the boxes and puts the flower in HIS button hole.)

There!

(WALTER and CHRIS face each OTHER for a long moment. It is a loving and tender moment.)

Happy wedding day, Daddy.

WALTER

Happy wedding day, baby.

(CHRIS kisses WALTER'S cheek, and THEY hug warmly.)

CHRIS

(Breaking away.)

We're almost ready. Daddy, you take the suitcases.

(WALTER exits into hall L and returns with two suitcases. CHRIS starts to exit.)

Dorine, you take Mother on out. Have we forgotten anything? Jenny, my bouquet....

JENNY

Go on. I'll bring it.

DORINE

(Leading LENA into the kitchen.)

Come on, Lena. We goin' to a weddin'.

LENA

Is it our wedding day?

DORINE
That's right, honey. You come along now.

CHRIS
Dorine, get Mother into the car. Daddy, take those suitcases on out.

JENNY
You go ahead. I'll close up.

DORINE
(To LENA.)
Come along, honey.

LENA
When we get to the church, Walter is going to marry me. And this time, we are going to be happy.

(For a moment, ALL are stricken by what LENA has said. WALTER slowly exits by the porch, carrying the suitcases.)

DORINE
Come on, Lena. It's Christine getting' married today.

(CHRIS stands as if afraid to move forward as DORINE and LENA exit.)

JENNY
It's all right. Go on now. It's all right...! Remember: This is your happy day.
(CHRIS exits. SPOT UP on JENNY, who stands, holding the bouquet, intently trying to weave a spell.)
Weave a circle round her thrice,
And close your eyes with hold dread,
For she on honey dew hath fed,
And drunk the milk of paradise.

(UPSTAGE LIGHTING FADES. SPOT on JEN-
NY fades. SPOT UP on JENNIFER DL.)

JENNIFER

I am he that walks with the tender and growing night,
I call to the earth and sea half-held by the night,
Still nodding night – mad naked summer night,
Smile, for your lover comes.

(JORDAN enters and stands behind JENNIFER, his arms around her as she looks out over the heads of the audience.)

Oh, Jordan, do you remember the night we walked by the park? It had been raining, and the streetlights were glowing in the mist. And as we walked, we made the world anew, like gods, from rain and mist and night and joy. And I said, "Promise that you'll never forget this moment. Listen—it is the happiest moment of my life whatever comes. I have loved and been loved and that can never change. Promise you'll remember when I loved you with all my heart. It was night. We were walking by the park, And the streetlights were glowing in the rain.

(THEY exit together, HIS arm around HER.)

SLOW FADE to BLACK.

END OF SCENE ONE

ACT II: SCENE TWO

(LIGHTS Up to dim on main set. It is evening, just after supper. The mood and condition of the Kraus household indicate that time has passed. The household has a run-down appearance. LENA is standing in the kitchen, staring out over the audience as through a window. DORINE is at the sink washing and drying the last of the supper dishes. WALTER is sitting on the sofa in the living room. A whiskey bottle and a glass are on the coffee table before him, and a cigar is smoldering in the ash tray. He continues to take frequent sips of the whiskey. LENA and WALTER are much more disheveled in appearance. DORINE is dressed, as before, in a much-laundered blue uniform.)

DORINE
(Finishing at the sink and drying HER hands.)
Guess I done diaperin' that baby.
(DORINE crosses to LENA.)
Lena, don't you want to come on in and sit down? I put the rest of the supper in the icebox in case Walter want hisself some.
(DORINE takes LENA gently by the arm and starts to lead her into the living room and helps her to sit in a rocking chair.)
Here, sit down, Lena.
(To Walter.)
Walter, you better let me fix you some supper 'fore I go.

WALTER
(In a thick, drunken voice.)
Just go on and go.

DORINE
You better eat somethin' or that whiskey goin' to eat up you insides.

Walter! You got to pull youself together. Ain't no use you carryin' on like this.
> (Picking up a letter from the coffee table.)

Walter, you ain't opened this here letter from Christine.

WALTER

Christine?

DORINE

Yes, this here letter Christine done sent. It come this mornin'. You want me to open it for you?

WALTER

> (Snatching the letter from her.)

If I want it opened, I'd of opened it.

DORINE

No use you tearin' you self up. She got a good husband and a nice home. She done gone and you got to make the best of it. The good Lord give us all our cross to bear and we got to make the best of it.

WALTER

Go on, if you're going.

DORINE

I'm goin'.
> (Muttering aloud but mostly to herself.)

You cain't go on this away. No, sir. Cain't go on this away.
> (DORINE puts out the cigar smoldering in the ash tray.)

Leavin' this here cigar layin' round, you goin' to set the whole house on fire.
> (SHE gives the coffee table a half hearted dusting with her hand.)

This place need a good cleanin', but I cain't do everything. No, sir. I cain't do everything, Lord. I only got two hands. You want anything 'fore I go, Walter?

(WALTER pretends he doesn't hear her.)
Clarence'll have a fit if I don't get on home and fix his supper. You better eat youself some supper, Walter. I left it in the icebox.
(WALTER does not answer.)
Lena, I'm getting' ready to go. See you all in the mornin'.

(DORINE exits through the shop door at R. LENA continues rocking catatonically, her head tilted far back, staring.)

WALTER
(Calling into the kitchen.)
Christine!—Christine! Get on out here!
(After an impatient pause, HE gets up in a drunken daze and staggers into the kitchen, carrying the letter from CHRISTINE.)
Christine!

(HE crosses toward the hall L and then, remembering that CHRISTINE is gone, makes a gesture of rejection and crosses to the table where HE sits dejectedly, throwing the letter on the table. JENNY enters DR as JENNIFER enters DL. BOTH face WALTER. SPOT UP to DIM on JENNY and JENNIFER. In JENNIFER'S DREAM, WALTER rises and moves away from the table, HIS back to the audience. HE has now taken on the persona of JENNY/JENNIFER'S FATHER.)

WALTER as JENNY'S FATHER
So you finally decided to come home!

JENNY
Daddy, there's something I want to tell you. I'm pregnant. Paul and I are going to have a baby.

WALTER as JENNY'S FATHER
What are you telling me? You got married to that boy you brought down here! Against my wishes! And now you're pregnant?

JENNY
Yes.

WALTER as JENNY'S FATHER
His father's a common factory worker! That's the kind of family you married into! Just like that friend of yours! Common as dirt! That's the kind of family you married into! I told you! And you didn't listen! You never listen!

JENNY
I knew you'd act like this! I knew what you'd say! I knew you'd get angry! You're always angry!

WALTER as JENNY'S FATHER
It's not too late. You can have this marriage annulled.

JENNY
No, I can't! Didn't you hear what I said? I'm pregnant! I'm going to have his child!

WALTER as JENNY'S FATHER
My God! Do you know what you've done?

JENNY
Aren't you even happy that I'm going to have your grandchild?

WALTER as JENNY'S FATHER
Do you know what you've done? You've thrown your life away on that boy! On that family!

JENNY
Do you know what you've done? I could never expect you to understand! Oh, leave me alone! Leave me alone!

                    WALTER as JENNY'S FATHER
Leave you alone? You're 18 years old! You haven't graduated from college! He has no education! No job! Whose money will you live off of?

                              JENNY
Not yours! I don't want your money! Do you think I can be bought and sold? Do you think you can order me around like you do mother? Do you think you can slap me around like you do her?
             (WALTER as JENNY'S FATHER slaps JENNY in
             the face. She stands glaring at him.)
I hate you! I hate you! I never want to see you again!

                    WALTER as JENNY'S FATHER
Jenny—I'm—sorry—I....

             (HE reaches out to HER.)

                              JENNY
Don't touch me! I will never forgive you for this! Never! As long as I live, I will never forgive you!

             (The light DIMS on WALTER, who sits at the
             kitchen table. JENNY exits. CHRIS enters.)

                            JENNIFER
When my father was in the hospital, dying, my mother called me to come home, but I didn't go.
             (A phone RINGS. CHRIS and JENNIFER answer
             the phone.)
Mother, how are you...? How is Dad?

                              CHRIS
Dorine...? Yes, I'm fine. How is Dad?

                            JENNIFER
Mother, I can't come home.

CHRIS
Dorine, I can't come. I can't bear to see them the way they are.

JENNIFER
Mother, you know how he was when I went to visit him in the hospital. There was a solid wall of ice between us—too cold, to ever break through.

CHRIS
Oh, Dorine, there's nothing I can do to change them.

JENNIFER
There's nothing I can do or say to change it. Mother, I can't come home. He doesn't even want me there.

CHRIS
Dorine, I'm sorry. I love you. Goodbye.

JENNIFER
Mother—I'm sorry. I love you. Goodbye.

CHRIS
I never saw my father again. I never said goodbye.

JENNIFER
Not even for my mother's sake would I go home. I never saw my father again. I never said—goodbye.

(LIGHTS on JENNIFER and CHRIS FADE. JENNIFER and CHRIS exit. WALTER, sitting at the kitchen table, picks up Chris' letter.)

WALTER
There you are! In a goddamn letter!
(HE manages to rip open the envelope and remove the letter, and then unsteadily tries to make out what it says.)

"Dear Daddy...." Shit!
> (HE reads and then suddenly stops, staring at the letter, then letting it fall.)

She's going to have his baby.
> (Calling loudly in Lena's direction.)

Do you hear? She's going to have his baby!
> (LENA, rocking in the chair, does not respond.)

Christine!—Christine!

> (WALTER slumps at the table in an attitude of despair. Lighting changes to a SOFT light. LENA rises and crosses. SHE is no longer the somnambulist. SHE is HER youthful self.)

LENA

Walt?—Walt?

> (WALTER rises and crosses to LENA. HE, too, has become HIS younger self.)

WALTER

Len—come out.

LENA

Walt, hold me. I'm afraid.

> (WALTER takes LENA in his arms.)

WALTER

There's nothing to be afraid of. I'm here with you.

LENA

Oh, Walt.

WALTER

I want you always to be like you are tonight. Promise me that you'll stay just as you are. Promise that you'll never change.

LENA
I promise. Walt—can it be a sin to be happy?

WALTER
No, it isn't a sin. I want you always to be happy.

LENA
They think it is a sin to dance. It can't be a sin, can it, Walt?

WALTER
Nothing that makes us this happy can be a sin.

LENA
Will we go to hell for being happy in each other's arms?

(WALTER takes HER in his arms.)

WALTER
No. I want you to be happy.

(LENA withdraws from WALTER's arms.)

LENA
I'm afraid when I'm happy! Afraid I'll be punished! That it's not right! That it's a sin to be so happy! That it's sinful to make love!

WALTER
(Gently.)
Len, it's all right.

LENA
When you're not here, I'm afraid

WALTER
You don't need to be afraid. I'm here.

LENA
Afraid I'll never see you again. I'd die—if I never saw you again.

WALTER
Don't be afraid. I'm here. I won't leave you.

LENA
If I come with you, will you marry me?

WALTER
Oh, Len, I love you. I want you to be with me.

LENA
The only time I feel safe is when I'm with you. Will you keep me safe?

WALTER
Yes, I'll keep you safe.

LENA
Promise?

WALTER
Yes, I promise.

LENA
(Turning away with HER back to HIM. Moving away from HIM.)
Walter—I think I'm pregnant.

WALTER
I'm glad. They'll have to let us marry now.

LENA
I don't know what it will be like. All the blood and the pain. I don't want to have a baby!

WALTER

It will be all right.

LENA

I'd kill it if I could!

WALTER

(HE goes to HER and tries to hold HER, but HER body is stiff, and SHE pushes him away.)

You don't really mean that. I'll be there with you. I won't leave you. I promise.

(Lighting DIMS. SHE moves away from HIM. WALTER now stands by HIMSELF as if gently holding a baby in HIS arms.)

Look, she's a beautiful baby.

LENA

No! Take it away! I don't want it! There's something wrong with it!

WALTER

She's as healthy as any baby can be. She's a beautiful baby.

LENA

No! Take it away! I don't want to ever see it again! I wish it had died! I wish it was dead!

WALTER

Sh–h–h–h, don't say that, Len. You don't mean that. It will be all right.

(HE reaches out to touch HER.)

LENA

(Pulling back.)

Don't touch me! Don't ever touch me again! I can't stand you to touch me! It's disgusting! I feel dirty! There's blood all over me! All over me!

(Suddenly SHE makes a threatening gesture toward

                    WALTER's sheltering arms.)
I'll kill it! I'll kill it!

                         WALTER
                    (Fending HER off.)
Len! Len!
                    (LENA retreats, like an animal at bay, into the darkening living room.)
Len!
                    (LENA sits in the rocking chair but does not rock. WALTER looks down at the baby in his arms.)
Sh–h–h–h–h, don't cry now, Christine. Everything will be all right. You'll see. I'll keep you safe. Sh–h–h–h, now. You're the prettiest baby in the whole wide world. There now. Don't cry. Everything will be all right.
                    (Downstage LIGHTS FADE. LIGHTS UP to DIM on main set. WALTER crosses to the sofa and sits on the sofa. He lights a cigar. LENA is now rocking in the rocking chair)
Stare! Stare! Stare! Don't you ever close your eyes, you ugly bitch? You sleep with your eyes open like a horse! And you smell like one! You crazy bitch! What kind of wife are you? I wish you were dead! Do you hear? I wish you were dead! I wish we both were dead!

                    (HIS body slumps. He lies down, glowing cigar in hand. Almost immediately he falls into an alcoholic slumber. LENA continues rocking, staring aimlessly. SMOKE rises from the sofa. LENA does not respond to the smoke at first, but as it becomes heavier, she stops rocking and focuses on WALTER. Slowly, she rises and takes a few steps toward the sofa. FLICKERS of FLAME seem to be seen in the thickening smoke.)

                         LENA
                    (Hesitantly.)
Walter!—Walter!

WALTER
(Stirring, but not awakening.)
Christine!—Christine!

(LENA stands staring at WALTER for another beat or two, then moves stiffly, awkwardly, to the kitchen area where SHE stands, staring out over the heads of the audience.)

BLACKOUT

END of SCENE TWO

ACT II: SCENE THREE

(The Kraus living room. The LIGHTING simulates the ambiance of a dull, DREARY DAY. Packing boxes are scattered around. The living room furniture UR has been removed. LENA is sitting silently at the kitchen table, staring into space. DORINE is sitting at the table, sewing. BOTH LENA and DORINE are wearing dark dresses.)

CHRIS
(Entering from hall UL.)
Dorine, I should have helped with those dishes.

(CHRIS seems older, more mature. SHE is 20 years old. SHE is wearing a simple dark dress and medium high heel shoes.)

DORINE
There weren't that many. I jus' thought I'd sew these here buttons on Lena's coat while we're waitin'. They all ripped off.

CHRIS
(SHE hugs DORINE.)
I don't know what I would have done these last weeks without you!

DORINE
That's all right, Honey.

(CHRIS starts to pack dishes from the cupboard into a carton. JENNY enters by the porch. SHE is carrying an umbrella and a box of cookies. JENNY, too, is older and more mature. SHE is 18 years old. HER clothes, stockings, and medium heels indicate that time has passed.)

JENNY

Chris? Are you here?

CHRIS

Jenny? Come in! That wind is turning cold.

JENNY

It's starting to rain.
    (JENNY lowers the umbrella, and JENNY and CHRIS hug.)
I'm sorry about your father, Chris

CHRIS

Thank you. The flowers you sent were beautiful.

JENNY

I'm sorry I couldn't go to his funeral. It was just—too many funerals—my father and now yours.

CHRIS

I know. We've had our share of funerals. How are you feeling?

JENNY

I'm all right.
   (To DORINE and LENA.)
Hi, Dorine. Miz Kraus.

(LENA does not acknowledge JENNY'S greeting.)

DORINE

My, Jenny! You all growed up.

JENNY

Yes, I guess so.

DORINE

I'm sorry 'bout you Daddy and you losin' the baby. That's real hard.

JENNY

Yes. Thank you, Dorine.

DORINE

When the Good Lord call, we got to go.

JENNY
(Giving DORINE the box of cookies.)
Mother thought Miz Kraus might like some of Lafronia's cookies to take with her.

DORINE

Tell her thank you. Lafronia is a real good cook.
(To LENA.)
Lena, do you want a cookie?

(LENA does not respond.)

JENNY

Miz Kraus, Mother said to tell you she's going to come and visit you.

(LENA does not respond.)

DORINE

Tell you mother, that will be real nice.

CHRIS

Dorine, would you take her into the bedroom, so Jenny and I can talk?

DORINE

Sure, honey.

(DORINE gathers up the coat and sewing basket and leads LENA into the upstage bedroom. JENNY turns to CHRIS and holds her at arm's length, intently looking into her face.)

JENNY
You're pale.

CHRIS
Am I?

JENNY
You need some color in your cheeks.
        (JENNY pats CHRIS' stomach.)
You're not beginning to show, yet.

CHRIS
No, not yet.

JENNY
How does Frank feel about being a father?

CHRIS
He thinks it's great. We were afraid I'd never get pregnant. His parents are really looking forward to their first grandchild.

JENNY
Yes.

CHRIS
How is Paul?

JENNY
He's—all right. Where is Frank?

CHRIS
He went on out to see that everything is ready.

JENNY
Did he find a buyer for the shop?

JENNY
Yes. Thank you, Dorine.

DORINE
When the Good Lord call, we got to go.

JENNY
(Giving DORINE the box of cookies.)
Mother thought Miz Kraus might like some of Lafronia's cookies to take with her.

DORINE
Tell her thank you. Lafronia is a real good cook.
(To LENA.)
Lena, do you want a cookie?

(LENA does not respond.)

JENNY
Miz Kraus, Mother said to tell you she's going to come and visit you.

(LENA does not respond.)

DORINE
Tell you mother, that will be real nice.

CHRIS
Dorine, would you take her into the bedroom, so Jenny and I can talk?

DORINE
Sure, honey.

(DORINE gathers up the coat and sewing basket and leads LENA into the upstage bedroom. JENNY turns to CHRIS and holds her at arm's length, intently looking into her face.)

JENNY
You're pale.

CHRIS
Am I?

JENNY
You need some color in your cheeks.
            (JENNY pats CHRIS' stomach.)
You're not beginning to show, yet.

CHRIS
No, not yet.

JENNY
How does Frank feel about being a father?

CHRIS
He thinks it's great. We were afraid I'd never get pregnant. His parents are really looking forward to their first grandchild.

JENNY
Yes.

CHRIS
How is Paul?

JENNY
He's—all right. Where is Frank?

CHRIS
He went on out to see that everything is ready.

JENNY
Did he find a buyer for the shop?

CHRIS

He thinks so, if Dorine is willing to stay on. She's the one who's kept the shop going. I don't know what I would have done without her.

JENNY

Does your mother know—about the hospital?

CHRIS

She doesn't know anything.

JENNY

Maybe you should tell her—before you go.

CHRIS

I can't—I can't talk to her at all. She doesn't understand anyhow.

JENNY

How long do you think your mother will have to stay—out at the mental hospital?

CHRIS

How long? Why do you ask?

JENNY

I remember what you said about your father. That he would never put her away. That he would always keep her at home.

CHRIS

Home? Where is her home?

JENNY

I guess—it's with you now.

CHRIS

With me? This isn't my home! I hate this place! I have a home of my own and now my own family to take care of. I don't care what happens to her!

JENNY
Oh, Chris, you can't mean that!

CHRIS
Then you don't know me very well.

JENNY
Your mother is your family, too! She hasn't got any family but you.

CHRIS
Family? What kind of family has she ever made for me? I've had to hang my head in shame everyday of my life for what she's done to me! Family! Oh, my God! Family!
(JENNY cannot hide a disapproving look.)
Don't look at me like that! Don't you understand? I would end up as crazy as she is! Staring at the walls. Waiting to die. I know that feeling! I've got to get away from here, I've got to get away from her!

JENNY
Oh, Chris, your mother doesn't know what she's doing!

CHRIS
That's not true. I know her. There's a part of her that knows what's going on and hides behind the craziness. It must be easy to be crazy and not have to bear the burden of everything! It must be an easy way out!

JENNY
Oh, Chris, it can't be easy. It can't ever be easy.

CHRIS
You don't know her as I do. The whole house would have burned down if the neighbors hadn't seen the flames in the window. I don't want her with me, ever!

JENNY
Oh, Chris, I understand how you feel but....

(JENNY reaches out to touch CHRIS in a comforting way, but CHRIS jerks away from JENNY'S touch.)

CHRIS

You understand? How could you understand? Miss High and Mighty! How dare you judge me! You never had to put up with anything! It's always been so easy for you! You had a mother who worshipped the ground you walked on! And you had a father who saw to it you never had to want for anything! Well, where were you when your father was dying? Where were you? You didn't come home when your father was dying and calling for you!

    (CHRIS' emotions now building to near hysteria.)

How dare you judge me! How dare you be judge and jury all rolled into one and pronounce the sentence, "Guilty! Guilty! Guilty!"

    (CHRIS is acknowledging her own feelings of guilt and now turning anger at herself toward her mother.)

I can't stand the sight of her! When I look at her, a knife turns inside me so I can hardly breathe! I hate her! I can't stand to look at her for hating her so! All I can think of is that she should have been the one who died in that fire!

JENNY

Chris! She'll hear you!

CHRIS

Let her hear me! I want her to hear me!

    (CHRIS turns toward the upstage bedroom and begins to shout.)

You should have been the one who died in that fire! Not Daddy! You should have died!

DORINE

(Rising.)

Christine! Hush!

(LENA rises and moves to the bedroom steps.)

LENA
(Calling.)
Walter—Walter! Dorine, where is Walter?

CHRIS
Where is Walter?! Don't you know anything? He's dead! His clothes on fire! He burned to death! It should have been you who died in that fire, you idiot!

LENA
Yes. He called, "Christine—Christine," and I turned away.

CHRIS
(For the first time realizing what actually happened.)
You turned away? You did what?

LENA
He was on fire—in the smoke. I called, "Walter—Walter," and he said, "Christine."

CHRIS
You saw him on fire? You tried to wake him?

LENA
No, I walked away.

CHRIS
You knew he was on fire and you walked away?

LENA
I let him die. I killed him.

CHRIS
You killed him? You killed him?

(CHRIS suddenly attacks LENA.)

JENNY
(Grabbing CHRIS' arm.)
Chris, don't.

CHRIS
Wake up, you idiot! You killed him!

DORINE
(Stepping between CHRIS and LENA.)
Hush! For shame!

LENA
(As if in a trance.)
You killed him. He called, "Christine," and you let him die.

DORINE
Hush now. All you pain ain't goin' to bring him back.

CHRIS
(Turning on DORINE.)
You knew! You knew! Why didn't you tell me?

DORINE
You'd send her away jus' like you doin' now. She done have all the heartache she need in this life. She don't need no more from you.
(SHE looks at CHRIS for a long moment.)
Come on, Lena. We goin' to get ready to go.

(DORINE and LENA cross to the upstage bedroom where DORINE helps LENA put on HER hat and coat. As CHRIS breaks down, JENNY puts her arms around CHRIS and holds her.)

CHRIS
I—I don't want to look back. I see only pain. Daddy alone and drunk and his clothes on fire. What a horrible way to die! How could he stand it? He couldn't ever stand anything. He wasn't very

strong or brave, but I loved him. Oh, Jenny, she just stood there and let him die.

JENNY
Yes, she just let him die.

CHRIS
I've got to get away from her. That's the only chance I've got. Don't you see?

JENNY
Yes, I see.

CHRIS
When I leave today, I don't want to ever come back here again, or look back or remember any of this.

JENNY
We had some good times here, Chris.

CHRIS
Did we?

JENNY
I remember being happy here.

CHRIS
And I remember being unhappy.

JENNY
What about the fudge we used to make? And the garden we planted in the back yard? And the plays we used to put on in the old barn?

CHRIS
And no one came.

JENNY

It didn't matter. We were happy together, just to be alive.

CHRIS

Oh, Jenny, we were happy just to be together.

JENNY

Yes, we were happy.
>(After a pause, speaking quietly, not dramatically.)

Goodbye, Cyrano. Goodbye, my dream lover.

CHRIS

Goodbye, Daddy.

>(DORINE and LENA move from the bedroom to center stage. DORINE is carrying a suitcase.)

LENA

>(Stopping abruptly.)

Walter! Walter!
>(CHRIS and JENNY look at each other, helplessly.)

Dorine, where is Walter? Tell him it's time to go.

>(DORINE, LENA, and JENNY cross to stand in tableau at R. Lighting FADES on DORINE, LENA, and JENNY. SPOT RISES on JENNIFER DL and on CHRISTINE U Center. Throughout the following, neither look at each other.)

JENNIFER

>(Facing the audience.)

Christine? Christine?

CHRISTINE

>(The spirit of Chris.)

I am here.

JENNIFER

The house is so still. All of you are gone. All the people I knew and loved. All of you are gone. Oh, Christine, I dreamed of you again last night. I dreamed that I went into a railway station, down and down, flight after flight of stairs to the deepest level. A crowd was standing in a circle. As I drew near, the crowd parted, and I saw you lying on the ground, a babe lying in your arms. And I knew that you were dead. I knelt by your side, tenderly smoothing the winding sheet about you and the child, when you sat up, holding the babe in one arm, and I realized that you weren't dead but alive and happy! And you put your arm around me, and smiled, and I wept for joy. Oh, Christine, all those I loved, they are not lost.

CHRISTINE

No, we are not lost. We are here with you now.

JENNIFER

Christine, I didn't go to my father when he was dying. My mother called me. She begged me to come home, but I didn't go. Not even for my mother's sake would I go home. I let my father die, and I didn't go to him. At the end—he called my name.

FATHER'S VOICE (Off)

Jenny—Jenny.

JENNIFER

Father, forgive me.

CHRISTINE

My father loved me, and I let him die without me. At the end, he called my name.

FATHER'S VOICE (Off)

Christine—Christine.

CHRISTINE

Father, forgive me.

JENNIFER

I didn't go to you when you were dying. They said you were too weak to talk, too weak to hold a glass of water. That you prayed for death. And I didn't go to you. I couldn't bear to see you dying and all your dreams dying with you. Forgive me, Christine.

CHRISTINE

At the end, I let my mother die without me.
        (FAINT SPOT up on LENA and DORINE.)
Father, forgive me.

JENNIFER

Oh, Christine, why all the suffering and the joy and the pain?

        (FAINT SPOT UP on JORDAN standing UL and behind JENNIFER.)

CHRISTINE

That we live and love each other, for love endures even beyond the grave.

JENNIFER

That we live and love each other, for love endures even beyond the grave.

SLOW FADE to BLACKOUT

END OF SCENE THREE

END OF THE PLAY

Appendix

Dreamers, Shadows, Dreams
Workshops, Readings, and Awards and Honors

Workshops
1989, Downstage Theatreworks, Darien, Connecticut
1988, Sheboygan Theatre Company, Wisconsin

Readings
2002, New England Academy of Theatre New Play Series, New Haven, Connecticut
2000, The Schoolhouse Theatre Playwrights' Workshop, Croton Falls, New York
1991, Southern Appalachian Playwrights Conference, Mars Hill, North Carolina

Awards and Honors
2007, Semi-finalist, Trustus Theatre Playwright's Festival, South Carolina
2001, Chosen for New England Academy of Theatre New Play Series, New Haven, Connecticut
1991, Chosen for Southern Appalachian Playwrights' Conference, Mars Hill, North Carolina
1991, Finalist, Charlotte Repertory Theatre, North Carolina
1989, Chosen for Downstage Theatreworks New Play Series, Darien, Connecticut
1985, Finalist, Maude Adams Contest, Missouri
1983, First Runner-up, Southern Theatre Conference New Play Project
1983, Finalist, National Playwrights Conference, O'Neill Center, Connecticut

1983, Finalist, Jacksonville University Contest
1983, Finalist, Forest A. Roberts, Northern Michigan University

About the Authors

Jan Henson Dow has won more than 150 national playwriting competitions, awards, and honors, including an NBC New Voices Award. Her plays have received numerous productions, workshops, and staged readings around the country, and her full-length plays have been published by Samuel French and Popular Play Service.

As a Professor at Western Connecticut State University, Dow directed the Playwriting Workshops and co-produced Western's Festival of New Plays. She has been the recipient of a number of playwriting grants, as well as grants for the new play festivals. She also taught playwriting workshops at the Osher Life Long Learning Institute at the University of South Carolina and at workshops around the country. Her articles and poems have appeared in such publications as *The New York Times*, *The Dramatists Guild Quarterly*, *Kansas Quarterly*, and *Indiana Review*. She co-authored *Writing the Award Winning Play* with Shannon Michal Dow, and they have just completed their first novel, *The Darkest Lies*. Jan is a member of the Dramatists Guild.

Robert Schroeder has won a number of playwriting competitions, including an NBC New Voices Award. His plays have been staged nationally. He served on the staff of *The Dramatist Guild Quarterly* and the Dodd-Mead *Best Plays* reference annuals. His reviews and theatre commentaries also appeared in *The Nation*, *Commonweal*, *New York*, and other periodicals. His anthology, *The New Underground Theatre*, was published by Bantam Books, and he was among the contributors to *Playwrights, Lyricists, and Composers on Theatre*, a Dodd-Mead hardcover. He has been retained professionally as a play/musical "doctor" for a number of Off Broadway productions.

Phosphene Publishing Company publishes books and DVDs relating to literature, history, the paranormal, film, spirituality, and the martial arts.

For other great titles, visit
phosphenepublishing.com

1.1

www.ingramcontent.com/pod-product-compliance
Lightning Source LLC
Chambersburg PA
CBHW061442040426
42450CB00007B/1170